THE UNSILENT SOUTH

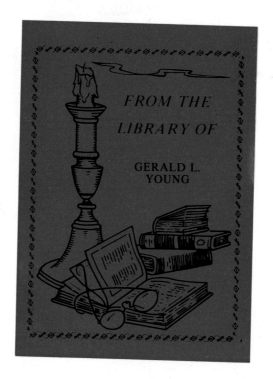

# THE
# UNSILENT
# SOUTH
## Prophetic Preaching in Racial Crisis
### EDITED BY
### DONALD W. SHRIVER, JR.

 JOHN KNOX PRESS
Richmond, Virginia

Dedicated to

ERNEST TRICE THOMPSON

and all others
who hunger and thirst after righteousness

LIBRARY OF CONGRESS CATALOG CARD NUMBER: 65-20546
© M. E. BRATCHER 1965
PRINTED IN THE UNITED STATES OF AMERICA
2645(20)8490

# Contents

# FOREWORD

The reading of this volume of sermons has been to me—as it will undoubtedly be to many others—a moving experience, stirring me at one and the same time to shame, pride, grief, and hope.

Shame there has been that such things could be. For in these sermons the curtain is pulled back; and we see something of the injustice which the white man has inflicted on the black man, things which all of us who live in the South have known, or should have known, but to which we have too long remained blind or indifferent.

Pride there is that these particular sermons were preached, and preached under the particular circumstances delineated by the editor; pride because running through them all is not only the warning of impending judgment and the call to repentance, but also the healing, reconciling word of God, along with the promise of mercy; pride in the knowledge that these sermons do not stand alone, that there are scores, hundreds of other ministers, many known to the writer, who in this or in other ways have sought to bring the disturbing, healing, reconciling word of God to bear upon the racial situation as it now exists in the South.

But there is also grief—grief for the Negro, for what he has endured, for what he is still called upon to endure; grief for the white man, a recognition of the inevitable judgment which he has brought and is still bringing upon himself and his children because of his continuing blindness; and grief for ministers—the price that faithful men have paid because in love they sought to bring home to their congregations the word of God which burned in their hearts. This story is only partly told in the pages that follow. There is the bare indication that a number of the preachers—four, to be exact—were forced out of their pulpits because of the words which they had spoken. But many of us know in detail the stories of ministers who, because of similar faithfulness, have suffered disappointment, frustration, the alienation of friends, rejection and hatred of their neighbors, disruption of congregations, economic pressure, harassment, and the threat of physical violence. And such experiences have by no means ended. Today's prophets are still being stoned by those who honor the tombs of the prophets of an earlier day (Matthew 23:29-31).

But mostly there is hope: hope because so often, as in many of the cases given here, the preached word has fallen on fertile ground; because it becomes clear that there is a Christian commitment in the South that needs only the fructifying word to produce its fruit; hope because many of the preachers in this series, though not all by any means, are young men, with the most of their ministry still ahead of them; hope because the sentiments here expressed are the sentiments of the vast majority of the young men now going out from our theological seminaries, the men who will be the pastors of tomorrow's churches as they are fast becoming the spiritual leaders of today's churches.

In these sermons there is new hope—for the white man and for the black man, for the church, for the South, and for the nation.

Ernest Trice Thompson

## ACKNOWLEDGMENTS

Most of these sermons have been shortened for publication, but each reads almost as it was preached. The prefaces were written with the help of the minister in each case, but only where he is quoted should he be charged with literal responsibility for the preface. By way of acknowledgments, I must state my enormous indebtedness to those in John Knox Press who encouraged this collection; to my wife, Peggy Leu Shriver, whose critical sensitivity has contributed as much to the substance of the work as her typing has contributed to its mechanics; and to those ministers of the Presbyterian Church, U.S. who graciously submitted manuscripts that do not happen to appear in the collection, but without whose witness the church would have much less reason to suspect that it is still the salt of the earth.


Donald W. Shriver, Jr.
*Raleigh, North Carolina*
*January 31, 1965*

# INTRODUCTION

In their study of the role of Little Rock ministers during the school crisis of 1957, Ernest Q. Campbell and Thomas F. Pettigrew came to the forthright conclusion that "the Protestant ministry is potentially the most effective agent of social change in the South in the decade ahead."[1]

Half of that decade has now passed—the half which began with the Greensboro sit-ins and which has ended with the first full year of the operation of the 1964 Civil Rights Act. In these five crucial years of the American Negro's struggle for first-class citizenship, have Protestant ministers in the South verified or refuted Campbell and Pettigrew's tentative, hopeful thesis?

The present volume should provide the reader with some materials for making his own judgment of the matter. At the same time, the volume does embody certain editorial judgments, and the reader deserves a statement of the standards governing the selection of contributions.

In general, the editor has sought to include sermons which singly and together suggest four dimensions of the southern minister's participation in the contemporary racial crisis. When he participates, he does so (1) as a person living in a certain region, (2) as a theologian, (3) as a human being subject to historical change, and (4) as a professional responsible for many facets of the life of a human community.

A word of explanation about each of these four is in order.

1. Numerous disturbances of the conscience and civil peace of America in the early nineteen-sixties have shown clearly that racism is a profound national illness. Yet these disturbances have also shown that the accents of spoken prejudice and the patterns of institutionalized discrimination vary from region to region throughout the country.

The persons whose words appear in these pages are peculiarly equipped to speak to the crisis of racial prejudice in one region of the nation: the South. Most of them were born and raised in the

South, all of them are now ministering in the South, and all are members of a denomination whose immediate past history is associated deeply with the South.

The denominational character of the collection needs some justification. Every person here speaks as a member of the Presbyterian Church in the United States, the so-called Southern Presbyterian Church. Various practical reasons might be given for the limitation of the collection to southern Presbyterians, but the major reason for the denominational limitation concerns southern regionalism itself. Alone among major American Protestant denominations heavily represented in the South in 1964, the southern Presbyterian church still maintains intact its approximate Civil War boundaries. As such, this denomination exemplifies an almost unique combination of nationalist and regionalist thinking. On the one hand, southern Presbyterians have not sponsored "home missions" in other parts of the United States, and they have consistently (though not without internal controversy) maintained their formal ties with the National Council of Churches.[2] On the other hand, they have not yet seen fit to unite organically with the so-called Northern Presbyterians (the United Presbyterian Church in the U.S.A.) from whom they were separated in 1861. Moreover, they have continued to maintain a peculiarly intimate tie between their feelings for their church and their feelings for the history of their region. They never quite forget that their denomination was born with the Confederacy but did not die with it. For them the Civil War is a part of "internal history" (as H. Richard Niebuhr would have said)[3] in a way which understandably baffles many observers from other regions. Historians have long probed this persistence of Civil War memories in the South—defeat nags the human memory longer than victory exhilarates it; a rural culture has a longer memory than an industrial culture; and the politics of anti-Reconstruction are slow to die— but whatever the reason, southerners still live in a band of time more or less periodized by the Civil War. The southern Presbyterian church is a major ecclesiastical expression of this periodization.

To focus on the travail of southern Presbyterian ministers in the midst of racial crisis, therefore, is to sample a larger cross section of the South than is immediately evident in the fact that in 1964 this denomination had only 944,716 members.[4] In this context one can describe the travail of the southern Presbyterian minister as akin to that of southerners in general, for he is a man raising questions such as these: How can one do justice to southern history while at the same time doing a justice and loving a mercy which sometimes have been conspicuously absent from that history? How can one execute the difficult maneuver of seeking to modify a culture while standing within it?

The sermons in this collection have been chosen partly on the basis of the skill with which certain southern Presbyterian ministers have formulated such questions for themselves and their congregations. And it will be obvious that their formulation implies the presence of a second skill: the use of theological leverage to modify one's cultural inheritance.

2. Dubbed a "teaching elder" by official church polity, the Presbyterian minister is expected to be a theologian. Some laymen in his congregation may utter the word "theology" with the headshaking accorded it by many other American Protestants; but John Calvin, the Westminster Confession of Faith, and modern educational requirements for ordination to the ministry combine to keep "theology" in reasonably good public standing in this denomination.

For this reason alone, if for no other, southern Presbyterians' ears were stung rather sharply by a forthright pronouncement of their 1954 General Assembly: "Enforced segregation of the races is discrimination which is out of harmony with Christian theology and ethics."[5] The impact of this single sentence upon the life of the denomination can never be measured, but it is probable that no other sentence from a General Assembly pronouncement has in recent times received such wide quotation in southern Presbyterian pulpits.[6] Yet that single sentence resounded strangely and shockingly in the ears of many because the sermons which had been preached to them in their youth had seldom connected the word "segregation" negatively with the word "theology."

The lack of such a connection was rooted in history. In the

nineteenth century, while the winds of liberal Protestant theology
were stirring in the North, southern Presbyterians were fashion-
ing a theological doctrine of the church which insulated it in principle from social problems. Called "the spirituality of the church"
by its friends, and "ecclesiastical docetism" by its enemies, this
doctrine for over a century asserted that the mission of the
church concerns the eternal salvation of souls rather than the
temporal salvation of society.[7] This antiseptic separation of
church from society, Christian ethics from social justice, is thor-
oughly un-Calvinistic, and it has little in common with that Presbyterianism which so largely supported the American Revolution.[8] But for a people whose historical consciousness has been
more attuned to the name Gettysburg than to the names Geneva
and Yorktown, this breakdown of Presbyterian tradition is understandable. (As one of the contributors to this volume points
out, this breakdown was made inevitable, perhaps, by the institution of slavery. In a society whose very economy depends upon
slave labor, a church that talked too openly about "social justice"
might have appeared hopelessly unrealistic and hypocritical.)

In short, the southern Presbyterian minister finds himself heir
to a tradition which imposes a quarantine on the mention of social
issues in church gatherings. To secure critical theological leverage on the most prominent of America's social problems in the
early 1960's, of course, he had only to grasp the Calvinistic and
biblical heritage at points neglected by his immediate theological
forebears. That many did learn to do so is evidenced by this volume. But to say how they learned to do so involves a consideration
of a third dimension of the minister's participation in the contemporary racial crisis: like other men, he is subject to the hustling of
history.

3. With their brethren in many other parts of the contemporary Christian church, the ministers who speak in these pages are
working out an understanding of the church which interprets
"spiritual" in a sense akin to "incarnate" and "historical." Indeed, many sermons in this collection were preached in partial
response to pressures nudging the preacher outside his study
door, to events which occurred in city streets and on riot-torn uni-

versity campuses. From one theological perspective, this characteristic of the sermons is a confession of the guilt of the Christian church, which has been rightly condemned in recent years as a "thermometer" rather than a "thermostat" of society.[9] From another theological perspective, however, it merely illustrates the history-reacting character of the church, which is as real as its history-making character.

That God speaks to his church partly through the world is not an idea which should ever have surprised Presbyterians, of course. The Westminster Confession of Faith, three-hundred-year-old creedal standard of most American Presbyterians, states sweepingly:

> "God, the great Creator of all things, doth uphold, direct, dispose, and govern all creatures, actions, and things, from the greatest even to the least, by his most wise and holy providence . . ."[10]

To entertain this awesome vision of the utterly sovereign God, as A. S. P. Woodhouse points out in his description of the Scotch-English Puritans who wrote the Westminster Confession, is to live "in a world of particular providences."[11] In such a world, what a man thinks and says inside a meetinghouse may depend partly on events occurring outside.

Woodhouse goes on to remind us that the discernment of God's providential will, especially for Puritans, was always a very complex matter. "Particular providences" were only one "mode" of God's instruction of his people. Apart from two other modes—the outward word of the Scripture and the inward experience of the Holy Spirit—the authority of events would have been unclear;[12] but mated with the study of Scripture and subjection to the Holy Spirit, contemporary events were not to be neglected by any spiritual son of Calvin. The word of God does not sound in a historical vacuum. The man who stands in the midst of men and nations learns best to say:

> "The lion has roared;
> who will not fear?

The Lord GOD has spoken;
who can but prophesy?" (Amos 3:8).

To the neglect of history southern Presbyterians laid themselves wide open as they fashioned the doctrine of the spirituality
of the church; and to the remedying of this neglect many of the
ministers in this volume have devoted no small part of their ministry. Most of the sermons show the marks of all three classic Puri-
tan modes of perceiving the will of God; but, precisely because
southern Presbyterians have neglected history more openly than
they have neglected Bible study and prayer, the editor has openly
sought to include in the collection a large number of sermons
whose vitality depends upon the minister's attempt to respond to
the pressures of the contemporary racial crisis. Some sermons
here may even suggest to the reader that under the impact of
events a minister is tempted to neglect the scriptural word and
thereby the word of the Spirit. It is the thesis of the collection,
however, that God empowers preachers through the Scripture,
through the Spirit, through the church, and through history in
their dynamic interrelationship.

Consistent with this thesis, each sermon in the book is pref-
aced by a description of the congregational, community, and
(sometimes) national context in which the sermon was preached.
Thus the reader will want to read these sermon-prefaces as carefully as the sermons themselves to remind himself that these
things were "not done in a corner."[13]

4. To take the historic and communal context of sermons seriously is also to take the extra-pulpit actions of preachers seriously.
In the Hebrew-Christian tradition, the distinction between word
and deed—even linguistically—is hard to determine. If the
breaking of the pulpit quarantine on social issues is an event in
southern history, then the distinction is doubly hard to make for
these sermons. Four of the ministers represented here lost their
pulpits in connection with their vocal witness on the racial question. Had their voices been safely insulated from influencing anything outside the bounds of their pulpits, these ministers would
doubtless have enjoyed continued job security. But in fact their
pulpit ministry was interlocked with many other facets of their

leadership of a congregation and a community, and the power of their spoken words depended in some measure on this.

The collection as a whole, therefore, raises the question of what it means for a Christian minister to act "responsibly" in the contemporary racial crisis. The word responsibility has rapidly come into vogue among Americans seeking the best name for the best of human actions. Perhaps the vogue has arisen because human action in our society has so many complexities. The minister has as much reason as any professional to be acquainted with these complexities. Perhaps he has more reason. In his pulpit, he builds his logical house on foundations which often seem only too alien to the marketplace; yet he professes a gospel that belongs to all in the marketplace. He feels responsible for interpreting the gospel to all. As the late W. Taliaferro Thompson liked to say, the minister's task is "to enable those for whom he is responsible to become Christian"—which is perhaps the most ambitious professional goal in the world, involving a man in an attempt to act justly and mercifully, truthfully and lovingly, boldly and humbly, as a prophet and as a priest, as a churchman and as a citizen, as a servant of all men and as a slave of none.

A manful attempt to bring into some realistic relationship these diverse facets of ministerial responsibility will be evident in many of these sermons. That their authors made such an attempt was the fourth and final standard for the making of the collection.

To the readers of these pages it will be apparent that such complexities belong to the vocation of many Christians besides ministers. Indeed, the editor suspects that most of the ministers represented here would soberly (and not just modestly or anxiously) reject Campbell and Pettigrew's evaluation of their potential role in southern society as "the most effective agent of social change." They would be the first to recognize, with social scientists themselves, the profound interdependence of the many agents of change in our time. This interdependence is so profound that the project of awarding a prize to one agent over another is inherently difficult, even on the level of social science. Indeed, to speak on the level which has priority for the writers of these pages, the ultimate prize must belong to no human agency at all. Presbyterianism gives God the glory.

# Amos Diagnoses
# Our Southern Sickness

John S. Lyles
Marion Presbyterian Church, Marion, South Carolina
October 13, 1957

The five ministers in this opening section are at one in their insistence that the scriptural word takes precedence over the word of southern culture. The sermon below, the only one from the nineteen-fifties, was preached from a pulpit that had already been lost because of this insistence.

Marion, South Carolina, is the county seat of Marion County, in the southeastern part of the state. Its population in 1957 was 7,000, evenly divided between white and Negro people. Economically the county depends chiefly upon tobacco, some cotton, and a few small industries.

The Marion Presbyterian Church was organized in 1852. Its membership of 335 includes business and professional people, a few farmers, and many community leaders. John S. Lyles became pastor of the church in September, 1955, when stormy protests to the 1954 and 1955 Supreme Court school decisions had begun to envelop the state of South Carolina. From 1955 to 1957, led by the state legislature and Governor George Bell Timmerman, Jr., the people of the state presented a generally unbroken front of opposition to all school desegregation. Talk of "state sovereignty" and "interposition" had been rampant in the legislature, which by 1957 had given broad new powers to the Governor "to do all and every act and thing which he may deem necessary in order to prevent violence or threats of violence."[1] Citizens Councils and the Ku Klux Klan continued very vocal

21

in many parts of the state; and in September, 1957, every public school in the state remained segregated.

In an atmosphere of stifled communication between the races and of intimidation directed toward "moderates," Mr. Lyles and four other South Carolina ministers, calling themselves "Concerned South Carolinians," joined quietly in an effort to persuade a group of widely respected South Carolina citizens to voice a moderate position in a small pamphlet to be entitled *South Carolinians Speak*. Said the prospectus for the pamphlet: "We desperately need the leadership of men and women who will debate the issues rationally, who will counter the voices of extremism with words of moderation, and who still have the humility and courage to see a goal in the future towards which we in South Carolina must be working gradually . . ."[2] Coming into possession of a copy of this prospectus, Governor Timmerman made its contents public on July 3, 1957, and told reporters that "All South Carolinians, not just these self-appointed few, are 'concerned' South Carolinians."[3]

Immediately, *South Carolinians Speak* became front-page news. Away from Marion during the second week of July, Mr. Lyles returned to find that the elders of the Marion Presbyterian Church had met and decided that he had "disrupted the leadership" of the church and jeopardized his position as pastor. At the next official meeting of the session it was agreed that he would seek another pastorate.

In early September came the Little Rock school crisis. South Carolina newspapers were full of public leaders' praise for the actions of Governor Orville Faubus. On Sunday October 13, ten days before publication of the still unseen, much-maligned pamphlet, Mr. Lyles announced that he would preach two sermons on the subject of race relations. After hearing the first of these sermons, printed below, the session met with Mr. Lyles, and together they agreed to publish the following notice in the church bulletin of October 20: "Although the Session does not agree with Mr. Lyles' sermon last Sunday, we affirm his right to preach the Gospel as God leads him to do. However, because of present conditions in our church, and without in any way attempting to restrict the freedom of the pulpit, we have asked him not to preach his second sermon on race relations and he has concurred."

"The following week," says Mr. Lyles, "the pamphlet was published. There was mixed editorial reaction, complete silence from the Governor, and little comment by church members to me about it. I believe they were surprised by its mild tone."

A few weeks later the home of one of the twelve writers of the pamphlet, Claudia Thomas Sanders of Gaffney, was the target for a bomb. Like Mrs. Sanders, most of the writers had stressed a "slow but sure" approach to desegregation, with accent on the "slow."[4] One writer, Helen Burr Christensen of Beaufort, evaluated the current tension in South Carolina in positive and theological terms. Her comment is an apt introduction to the sermon below: "This tension, while unpleasant, is good, because it grows out of our unwillingness to practice the Christian ethic. . . . Basically, this is a Christian problem."[5]

Mr. Lyles is now pastor of the First Presbyterian Church, Virginia Beach, Virginia.

TEXT: AMOS 2:6-8; 3:1-2; 5:21-24

The prophets were never popular, because they declared judgment in the face of satisfaction. They demanded change in the presence of intrenched *status quo*. They looked beneath society's glittering surface to hidden sewers of immorality and injustice. Amos, a rugged shepherd from the barren shores of the Dead Sea, was such a prophet. He was a man who carried God's Word to a nation sick unto death, the kingdom of Israel.

Eighth-century (B.C.) Israel and twentieth-century South have much in common. There is outward prosperity, a peak of expansion, power, and influence. Religious activity is greater than ever: temples are jammed, altars are heaped high. Wide gaps show in the structure of society between two main groups: in Israel it was economic; in the South it is also color. Hear, then, Amos' message to Israel and his diagnosis of our southern sickness in race relations.

*God Executes Judgment.* Amos' first word was, "Thus says the Lord: 'For three transgressions . . . and for four, I will not revoke the punishment.' " God executes judgment. It falls upon all nations and peoples without favoritism. Based on moral principles, it is not capricious. That judgment is expressed in historic events. For some time, by various natural disasters (4:7-12), God had been nudging Israel, but they "did not return" to him. "Therefore thus I will do to you, O Israel . . ."

"Oh, Amos, quit sounding so pessimistic!" Within twenty years Samaria would lie in ruins.

"Oh, Jeremiah, God won't let Jerusalem fall!" In 587 B.C. the Holy City was completely smashed and the people carried into exile.

"Your Holiness, don't worry about that monk, Martin Luther!" In one decade the churches of all Europe had been shaken to their foundations.

God executes judgment! If he did not, the world would be utter chaos.

And so the first diagnosis: *our sickness is God's judgment on our sins against the Negro.* Those sins can be summed up in a word—enforced racial segregation. It is built on the myth of superior and inferior peoples. Merely because I was born white, I am "better"; he, born black, is innately inferior. It must be confessed that our denomination succumbed momentarily to this myth during the Civil War. In 1863 the General Assembly said in one report, "We hold the proper condition of the black is slavery." The next year, 1864, the Assembly declared, ". . . it is the peculiar mission of the southern church to conserve the institution of slavery." Our fathers in this synod once discussed a "selective breeding" policy to produce more valuable slaves. But the debate ended when a minister stated that slaves were property, not people, and so one might as well talk of marriage laws for cattle! These patterns of thinking led to mistreatment of the Negro, to financial exploitation, and to legal injustice. "For three transgressions and for four, O South, I will not revoke the punishment." That judgment has come, and what have we heard? "Political opportunists, Northern agitators, rabble-rousers, Communists!"

We have looked for excuses but not for God's hand of judgment. Nor have we really looked into our Bible. There is no biblical support for enforced racial segregation. There is no support for it in the Standards of the Presbyterian Church. There is no support in the history of the universal church. In 1865 our General Assembly finally said that "our churches, pastors, and people have always recognized this claim to Christian equality and brotherhood, and have rejoiced to have [the colored people] associated in Christian union and communion . . ." And only three years ago (1954) our Assembly affirmed "that enforced segregation of the races is discrimination which is out of harmony with Christian theology and ethics."

Thus I would be derelict as your pastor if I did not make it clear that our treatment of our fellow man—white and black—has eternal consequences for our souls. The kind of society we try to build must be explained to God. "We shall all stand before the judgment seat of God . . . each of us shall give account of himself to God" (Romans 14:10, 12). In that day how will our excuses sound? Which is more important, the approval of friends and society or the approval of the Lord God Almighty?

*Privilege Carries Responsibility.* Amos' second word from the Lord was, "You only have I known of all the families of the earth; therefore I will punish you for all your iniquities." Privilege carries responsibility. Little was expected of the pagan nations. But much was expected of Israel. God had chosen her, made the covenant with her, given her the land, defended her from enemies. She had had every opportunity. She had been chosen by the covenant. But she had twisted her election into a long orgy of self-indulgence. She had forgotten that she had been elected to serve God. When God dropped his plumb line in her midst, she did not measure straight. She had taken the materials of privilege and built an irresponsible society. So down she must come!

The second diagnosis: *we are sick because we have grasped privilege and refused responsibility.* Can anyone deny that the privilege has been all in our favor? Simply because we were born white, we had entrée to greater opportunities and advantages. Politically, economically, educationally, we have been privileged. And what of our responsibility? Either on the one hand we have borne it unwillingly: "We've done so much for them," or "They can't pay enough taxes"; or, on the other, we have refused to share responsibility with the Negro himself so that he, too, might become responsible. With almost a fifty percent Negro population in our state, how many Negro legislators are there? None. How many Negro mayors? None. How many Negro county, city, and state officials? A handful. There are many Negro Christians, capable and willing to serve. Let them share the responsibility along with their newly won privileges. If not, then let us quit complaining about the "white man's burden." "To whom much is given, of him will much be required" (Luke 12:48).

The church's performance has not been much better. In the so-called Bible Belt our Presbyterian church has some 900,000 members. And how many of those are Negroes? A little over 5,000—less than 1%! In South Carolina, with almost one million Negroes, less than five hundred are Presbyterian! We send missionaries to the ends of the earth to bring in people of every race, yet we have forgotten our responsibility right here at home.

*True Religion Means Social Justice.* Amos' third word is: "I hate, I despise your feasts, and I take no delight in your solemn assemblies. . . . But let justice roll down like waters, and righteousness like an ever-flowing stream."

Israel began as a religious nation, called into being by God, with the covenant as her constitution. From the outset she was to be a model of the community God wanted to create. Her worship and her common life were both living expressions of her fidelity to God. Priests and elders were the preservers of liberty and justice. God was just as concerned that men deal fairly with each other as that they worship him properly.

But men slipped into the blasphemous habit of thinking they could do what they liked as long as they placated God by gifts and sacrifices. So Amos railed at their false worship, saying that God wanted none of it. The reason Israel was destroyed was not that "religion" had gone out of fashion. The reason was that it was a man-pleasing religion rather than a God-obeying religion. Israel was destroyed because it cut out the religious heart, and the body died.

The third diagnosis is plain: *we are sick because we have tried to divorce religion from daily life.* This is not new in the church's history. In Bethel Presbytery, before the Civil War, one session suspended a man from Communion because he hired a coach and traveled on Sunday. Not one member of that church was ever suspended for breaking up a Negro home, selling the husband to one buyer and the wife and children to another. One session rebuked a slave when he suggested that Christians ought to do something about the plight of slaves. To break a "religious law" was a church concern, but violation of basic human justice was the individual's affair!

Some try to support this unholy separation of religion and life by using the misleading phrase "the spiritual mission of the church." Others feel that the church should not speak on this issue because it's controversial. What they often mean is "Don't speak, you'll upset vested interests," or "Don't speak because it will bring change." But Amos and our Lord Jesus knew nothing of such restrictions on the mission of the church. Where people and their relationship to each other are at stake *the church must speak*. If she doesn't, she deserves no more respect than a physician who withholds medicine and lets a patient die.

Christianity means social justice for all people, white and black. Do you remember those terrifying words of Jesus? "Depart from me, you cursed, into the eternal fire prepared for the devil and his angels; for I was hungry and you gave me no food, I was thirsty and you gave me no drink, I was a stranger and you did not welcome me, naked and you did not clothe me, sick and in prison and you did not visit me" (Matthew 25:41-43). Here the standards of judgment are not religious activity but actual deeds of kindness and love.

This is Amos' diagnosis of his society and ours: we are being judged for our sins; we have taken privilege and shrugged off responsibility; we have tried to separate religion from social justice. And we are sick.

God has brought us to this hour. In our sickness he is at work. In the midst of turmoil he is calling his people to stand firmly for justice, equality, and love. From this sickness our church and the South will either recover and move into a period of robust good health in race relations or go into a relapse whose course cannot be predicted. Which way the South responds to her sickness will depend primarily on the *witness* and the *actions* of southern white Christians.

May God give all of us humility to accept his healing and strength to follow his will.

# *And in Samaria?*

James Peck
First Presbyterian Church, Enterprise, Alabama
February 10, 1962

The town of Enterprise is in southeastern Alabama, forty miles north of the Florida line. Its major "industry" is Fort Rucker, a U. S. Army aviation training post; and its population of about 13,000 is somewhat transient. Businessmen, professionals, and a few farmers make up most of the permanent white residents of the town. Some thirty percent of the community is Negro.

The First Presbyterian Church has for many years consisted of a small nucleus of permanent residents and a larger transient membership of Army-related families. Transiency has kept the membership totals to about one hundred over the past few years, but it has also made the congregation more cosmopolitan than many other southeastern Alabama churches. The relation between permanent residents and military families has been the occasion of congregational friction. In 1959 a dissatisfied group of members, composed of persons hoping to carry on a vigorous ministry to military personnel, formed a second congregation.

James Peck became pastor of First Church in the summer of 1961, soon after his graduation from seminary. "Aware of the recent storm in the congregation," he remembers, "I was especially interested in a healing ministry in Enterprise." Indeed, a year later, the Session of First Church wrote a letter of confession and repentance to the alienated congregation, asking forgiveness for their contribution to the split and inviting the second church to discuss a merger on a basis of complete mutuality. Unfortunately, the letter was never answered.

The present sermon, preached eight months after the beginning of his pastorate, was delivered on Race Relations Sunday, 1962. It was

Mr. Peck's only sermon during three years which dealt focally with the issue of racial discrimination. No vocal objections to the sermon were expressed by the congregation at the time. But almost a year later, after Mr. Peck had written a letter to the Montgomery *Advertiser* expressing disagreement with a published letter from a segregationist Presbyterian minister, his elders counseled him to say nothing more about race relations. Soon afterward, as the tempo of the Negro protest movements quickened all over the United States, an unfounded rumor was spread in Enterprise that Mr. Peck was "arranging a sit-in" in his own congregation. "People were afraid of shadows," recalls Mr. Peck, "and local ministers were warning people that the NAACP was about to swoop down upon them." In response to the rumors, the session adopted an open-door policy for the seating of possible Negro worshipers. The policy contained the qualification that if a Negro came, the minister would not extend his usual welcome to visitors from the pulpit nor would he greet worshipers that Sunday at the door. The policy was never tested.

From this time on, membership and attendance dwindled, among both permanent and transient residents. An increasing number of persons openly stated that the minister's views on race were the cause of their leaving, and some stated that the sermon in February, 1962, had been the turning point of their relation to him. A common complaint was that these views could have only a bad effect on "stewardship and membership."

In these circumstances, Mr. Peck requested East Alabama Presbytery to dissolve the pastoral relationship between him and the congregation on June 1, 1964. The presbytery acceded to the request, and for three months he was without employment. He is now head of the Bible department and professor of New Testament at the Westminster Schools in Atlanta, Georgia.

## TEXT: JOHN 4:9; JOHN 8:48; LUKE 10:25-37; ACTS 1:8

In a letter commending the *Presbyterian Survey* for its bold editorial policy, a minister said, "I don't know how you get away with some of the things you print. Yes, I do, too; the church honestly wants it and we have underrated and underfed our people."

We ministers have, by and large, underrated the desire of our people to hear the whole story and to adjust their opinions and behavior according to the Word of God. One reason we find the church at times so covered with moss and so embarrassingly out of the picture is that ministers—we might as well admit it—have been afraid of shadows and ghosts and goblins.

As the writer of Hebrews would say, "I am persuaded better things of you, brethren." I believe you want to hear with respect what the church has to say. And it is in that confidence that I approach my subject. Your opinions and mine may never become identical, but that isn't of prime importance. What is important is that we have soberly wrestled with the Word of God on a very crucial issue of life, in a spirit of love and understanding. I trust that it is in this spirit that we now proceed.

We must go first to the Holy Scriptures as our final court of appeal in race relations. As Dr. Ben Lacy Rose has said, "The course which the church follows in this matter . . . should not be determined by the prevailing traditions and customs of the secular society in which we live; nor by the feelings of the majority of the church members; nor by what seems to us to be wise, or timely, or expedient; nor by what promises the least strife in or disaffection from the membership; nor by what appear to us to be the consequences, desirable or undesirable, of our chosen course. The course which the church follows in this matter should not finally be determined even by the Supreme Court of these United States, for we acknowledge a higher authority. *Our sole authority on this matter is God's inspired and infallible Word.* . . . Our problem is to discover and then strive to conform the life of the church to the practice and principles of the Bible."[1]

The selected passages which I have read from the Bible have to do with Jesus and the Samaritans. Professor Joachim Jeremias reports that just prior to the birth of Jesus the ancient hostility between Samaritans and Jews had grown into "a burning hatred." About A.D. 8 this hatred broke out "with renewed bitterness. Now the Jews forbade marriage and trade with the Samaritans whom they stigmatized as a mixed race, and in matters of religious observance placed them on a level with Gentiles. This was the situation in the time of Jesus as the gospels bear witness . . . and 'Samaritan' is a term of reproach (John 8:48) by which the

Jews express the depth of their contempt for the bastard race."[2]

In John 8:48 this is apparent; Jesus had just said some very disturbing things to a group of Jewish churchmen, and they derisively retorted by calling him a "Samaritan." When they couldn't think of anything worse to call him, they called him a Samaritan. This usage was for them a parallel to our popular terms of disrespect, "nigger," or "nigger lover" (which terms, I pray God, will soon be abandoned by all Christian people).

In another place, John 4:9, Jesus has met a Samaritan woman beside a well and has asked her for a drink of water. She is shocked and amazed that he would have anything to do with her, and she answers, "How is it that you, a Jew, ask a drink of me, a woman of Samaria?" And the Gospel writer adds, "For Jews have no dealings with Samaritans." It is obvious to the woman, and to all who read the story, that Jesus has violated social custom. He has not refused to drink at the same water fountain with a member of the out-group, with the result that an entire town was given the Word of God!

Again, in Luke 10:30-37, Jesus tells the parable of the Good Samaritan, which is so familiar to us. The story is told in answer to the question: "Who is my neighbor?" Jesus deliberately chooses to make the hero of his story a Samaritan, who sets up a makeshift integrated medical clinic to care for an injured Jew.

Finally, in Acts 1:8, the Risen Lord sends forth his disciples specifically to minister among the despised race of Samaritans. "Ye shall be witnesses unto me both in Jerusalem, and in all Judaea, *and in Samaria,* and unto the uttermost part of the earth" (K.J.V.).

Thus we see it in the Bible. Tradition and contemporary society demanded one thing, and Jesus openly disregarded it. We may be certain that the Jewish leaders had not forgotten this when they clamored for his crucifixion.

Before we turn to the significance of the embittered relation of Jews and Samaritans to our own society, may I share with you a personal position? I have not made it a point to speak excessively on the race question since being here in Enterprise. I don't think I have avoided the issue when it has come up, but neither have I intruded it unnecessarily. I have wanted to give us ample time to get acquainted. I am suspicious of a firebrand just out of seminary who proposes to redeem the world before the ink on his diploma is dry. Also, I am aware that this church has had more than its share of hard knocks, and I have wanted to help lift the burden, not add to it.

But as a pastor I am convinced that it is unfair to remain silent about the chief moral question confronting many of my people. Before I came here in June of last year I prepared this general statement, which has been seen by some of you:

> I believe in the Lordship of Jesus Christ over all of life; over man's religion, man's tradition, man's opinion: and therefore must have freedom of the pulpit to proclaim this lordship as it shines through in the gospel. I am opposed to discrimination on the basis of race in any area of life, but especially in the church; and therefore would always seek to keep the doors of the church open to all who present themselves for worship there. I have promised the Presbyterian Church in the United States to study both the purity and peace of the church; and therefore will endeavor to lead God's people toward purity of outlook only in a spirit of peace and gentleness, yet firmness, after the example of Christ.
>
> I am convinced from the Scriptures that a minister must cultivate a loving consideration for the flock of God, for their personal, family, religious, and social feelings; and therefore will strive to know and respect the opinions that prevail, and to avoid forcing my own point of view upon those among whom I labor, and to avoid embarrassing them by irresponsible leadership.

This has been my position for several years, and is today.

To return to the reaction of Jesus to the Jewish-Samaritan problem, let us ask three questions of that reaction: What does this say to our missionary task? What does this say to our personal attitudes? What does this say to our life in society? Let us look first at the missionary task.

*The Missionary Task*. David Head, in his humorous little book entitled *He Sent Leanness,* caricatures our missionary prayers this way: "Bless all foreigners, but don't let them come to live next door. Bless all natives in foreign parts, and keep them there."[3]

I have interviewed several missionaries from Africa and Latin America, and almost without exception they complain that the greatest stumbling block to their work is the record of the home churches on race relations. Many Africans and Latin Americans are backward and uneducated, but they are not naïve. They can hear the uncertain sound that is made when a missionary has to speak out of both sides of his mouth.

And many times it is we who have to learn the lesson of generosity from those whom we seek to teach. Elizabeth Bowne, in her book *Gift From the African Heart,* records an old Liberian woman's thoughts on the matter: "Musing aloud she said, 'Even now those folks in Monrovia, they always act, well, like they better than us bush folks.' She shook her head sadly. 'I not understand. Some folks good, some folks mean. Some folks smart, some folks lazy.' She frowned. 'But I say folks is just folks everywhere. Dat what you say?' I glanced at her thoughtfully. It came to me that this humble little woman probably had never heard the words 'discrimination' and 'segregation.' I turned away from her and for a few moments I could not look again into her gentle eyes."[4]

Nor could I look again into such eyes. Could you?

*Our Personal Attitudes.* We who hope to be following Christ as disciples are constantly called to bring our personal opinions into conformity with his life and teaching. We are called to stand all of our old dogmatic notions in formation out in the sunlight and let the King of kings pass in review. No one will deny the difficulty of this. There is nothing more painful than exposing ourselves to possible correction. But the more stubbornly we resist, the more likely it is that we know our ideas will not stand the test.

The success which Jesus had in breaking with tradition can be attributed, in part, to the fact that he saw people as persons. He did not fall victim to the distorting business of generalization. No doubt he had met Samaritans who were lazy, dishonest, and smelly. But he never allowed himself to create stereotypes from these experiences. Each human being was a new human being for him. And, above that, his matchless love for all men prevented him from requiring everyone to be just as intelligent and hygienic and genteel as himself before he would associate with him.

Had Jesus wanted to, he could have protested that his forefathers had walked a certain path and therefore it was required of him; or he could have asserted that such and such racial views were expected of him by his friends and neighbors and business associates. But he could not bring himself to such easy rationalizations. For him the will of his heavenly Father was more important than the patterns of his grandmother; and the Kingdom of God stood above the Town Council, not below it.

*Our Life in Society.* I have already hinted that a Christian's personal convictions may be out of harmony with the cultural *status quo.* What, then, becomes the Christian's posture in society when his own loyalty to Christ declares him out of step with the crowd?

This also is a hard question. Obviously the Christian will not want to go around deliberately offending his friends and preaching down to those who have not seen as clearly as he has. He will be acutely aware of the damage done by irresponsible reformers. On the other hand, he will not want to hide his light under a bushel. He will want to say, humbly, with Luther, "Here I stand. I can do no less."

Let me suggest several guidelines for the Christian to follow in his social responsibility:

1. *Understand the Dilemma.* See the plight of our Southland in true perspective. Regardless of right or wrong in the past, we find ourselves in a confusing situation now. Badgered by hostile news media, misled by politicians, and prodded by our own consciences, we have been at a loss as to what to believe. Those of us from other sections of the country need to sympathize with this dilemma. We also need to understand the aspirations of the young Negro who feels thwarted in his effort at self-improvement. For him, "separate but equal" is always in the future. This is understanding the confused situation on a rather surface level, but this much is important if we intend to communicate together.

2. *Promote Respect.* Name-calling is childish for anyone. But for the Christian it is especially out of place. Untold good would be done if we eliminated such irksome terms as "kike," "wop," "nigger," "dago," "jig," "hunky," and "darky" altogether. Rather, let us use terms that are welcomed by the people to whom we refer. If we teach our children to say "ma'am" and "sir" to adults, we should teach them to do so to all adults.

3. *Seek and Share Information.* A person in genuine quest for truth cannot be satisfied with only that information which reinforces his prejudgments. We must read many books on the matter, listen thoughtfully, and share our insights with others.

4. *Avoid Regression.* Resist going back to old thought-forms that most people have discarded. Be thankful for the progress we have made. The Ku Klux Klan mentality has been repudiated by all level-headed leaders. Leave it buried, and do not mourn its passing!

5. *Pray!* "More things are wrought by prayer than this world dreams of."[5] You can prove this to be true even in such a realm as race relations. The chief privilege and obligation of the church, according to Karl Barth, is to pray for the troubles of the world.

A final word: Though we may not reach the point of crisis here for many years (but who knows?), we must be preparing ourselves and our children for progress in race relations—not steeling ourselves against that eventuality, not fortifying ourselves with myths, but arming ourselves with the mind of Christ. Hard days are ahead, and God is counting on the church to lead society, not to lag behind it. May God grant us convictions which honor our Christ, and grant us the courage of our convictions.

# The Worship God Wants

George A. Chauncey
First Presbyterian Church, Danville, Kentucky
October 14, 1962

Danville, county seat of Boyle County in central Kentucky, is a community of 9,000 persons. It is an old city, proud of its important role in the settlement of Kentucky ("the West") in the late eighteenth century. The principal industry is farming (tobacco is the money crop), but the city also has a few manufacturing plants. Located here are Kentucky State Hospital, the Kentucky School for the Deaf, the Christian Church's Children's Home, and Centre College, a Presbyterian-related coeducational school of almost six hundred students.

Negroes, comprising about fifteen percent of the population, live in belts of Negro housing scattered throughout the city. Job opportunities for them are severely limited. The only professional people are ministers or teachers. Danville High School was opened to Negro students on a voluntary basis in 1955, and a few Negroes elected to attend. The school system was not basically affected by the Supreme Court decision, however, until the fall of 1964, when a gradual plan of compulsory desegregation was initiated. There has been little organized protest against segregation among Danville Negroes, but most restaurants and theaters opened their doors to all patrons during 1962 or 1963. The motels opened their doors to all patrons after the 1964 Civil Rights Act was passed.

First Presbyterian Church, organized in 1784, stands on the edge of the Centre College campus. Its slightly more than four hundred members include farmers and faculty persons, merchants and professional people, young families and many retired folk. Like every other church in Danville except Second Presbyterian Church (U.P.U.S.A.), which has three Negro members, the church is segregated.

George Chauncey became pastor of the First Presbyterian Church in November, 1960. During an earlier pastorate in Arkansas, on the first day of the attempted desegregation of Central High in Little Rock, he joined two other ministers (Dunbar H. Ogden, Jr., and Will D. Campbell) to accompany Negro students through the crowds gathered before the school. "My role in that crisis," says Mr. Chauncey, "was a very minor one, but we were close enough to discover what mobs are like."

"The Worship God Wants" was preached in Danville as the fourth in a series of sermons on the nature of Christian worship in the fall of 1962 when newspapers were filled with stories of Oxford, Mississippi. The congregation was particularly interested in Oxford because one of its young ruling elders, a former professor at Centre College, had just joined the faculty of Ole Miss.

"At its first stated meeting following the preaching of this sermon," reports Mr. Chauncey, "the session declared the membership of the church open to all persons. Several Negroes have since visited for worship. A few months later several members of the congregation helped organize the Danville Council on Human Relations, a voluntary interracial and interfaith fellowship of over a hundred members. The Council now holds its semiannual meetings in the church. I am chairman of the Council, and three ruling elders are on its fifteen-member Board of Directors. The Council works quietly through informal conversations with restaurant owners, employers, school board members, and state legislators."

The culture of central Kentucky is more hospitable in some respects to a recognition of "the authority of the Word" as over against the authority of human culture than are certain areas of the deeper South; but the sermon and its situation suggest that even central Kentucky does not automatically drift under the authority of this Word. Like human authorities and human words, the Word of God must be asserted to be obeyed.

## TEXT: ISAIAH 58:1-12

Apparently a religious revival was going on in ancient Israel at the time when Isaiah 58 was written. People were coming to church as never before. Every Lord's Day both priest and ushers took great pride in the fact that they had almost a "full house." The choir was the largest and finest it had ever been. The anthems were truly magnificent. The various programs of the church were running smoothly. Even the financial contributions, though not as large as they should be, were coming in pretty well.

It was a religious revival, all right. And everyone was pleased. Everyone, that is, except the Lord. In spite of all the evidence of interest in religion, in spite of all the services and meetings, in spite of all the prayers and praise—the Lord was not pleased at all. So he raised up for himself a prophet and told him to get the loudest public address system he could find (to lift up his voice "like a trumpet") and to declare to his people in the midst of their religious revival the living Word of God.

The living Word of God, spoken in that day under those circumstances, is what is recorded for us in Isaiah 58. It is a word of protest, a word of proclamation, and a word of promise. Let us attend to that threefold word.

The Word of God proclaimed to ancient Israel was, first of all, a word of *protest*. The God whom those people worshiped protested against their worship of him. He protested against their worship because these sincerely religious people had yielded to that perennial temptation of sincerely religious folk—the temptation to separate prayer from politics, communion from the common life, the service of God from the service of men. What had happened was this: In their enthusiasm about what was going on in the church, they had ignored what was going on in the world. In their concern for religious fasting, they had neglected their neighbor's need for food. In their zealous attention to God, they had completely disregarded their brothers. And the Word of God to them was, "I'll have none of it! Fasting like yours this day will not make your voice heard on high."

There is no evidence at all in our text that these people were deliberately trying to deceive the Almighty. Other people at other times apparently did try to fool God with their worship. But there is no note of this callous contempt of God in the word that is before us. For these people do not scorn God. They ask for his judgment. They do not worship as a duty. They worship as a delight. They do not ignore their Creator. They seek him every day. Yet the Lord through his prophet still protests! And he protests because although they do not attempt to deceive him, they have succeeded in deceiving themselves. They have come, honestly and sincerely, to believe that real religion is a matter of prayer and praise, church attendance and institutional activity; and for the sake of his own integrity and their ultimate salvation, God simply can't let this stand! So, in effect, God says to them:

"Listen, as much as I rejoice in your worship, your praise, and your prayers, I cannot accept them apart from your faithfulness in the life of society. My interest is not in religion, but in life. I am not the God of the church, but the God of the world. And service to me, divorced from service to your fellow man, is not real worship at all. Fasting like yours this day will not make your voice heard on high" (see Isaiah 58:2-4).

Such is the divine protest which the church needs to hear in every generation, for the temptation to which ancient Israel yielded—the temptation to divorce love of God from love of neighbor—is the perennial temptation of the people of God.

The church in Russia yielded to this temptation. On the very day in October, 1917, when the Communist party seized control of the revolution in Russia, some key leaders of the Orthodox Church gathered for a discussion. And do you know what they discussed? Proper liturgical dress for the clergy! The church was in the midst of a social revolution, and its main concern was what robes its ministers should wear in church.

The church in Nazi Germany yielded to this temptation. Hitler did not persecute the church at first because at first the church was not in his way. It played right into his hands, either by endorsing what he wanted to do or by ignoring him through a separation of "civil" affairs from "religious" affairs. The persecution of the church in Nazi Germany began only after a small minority of courageous Christians insisted that this compartmentalization of life was a lie.

Has not the church in our own nation quite unintentionally yielded to this same temptation? We are now living in the midst of the greatest social revolution our nation has known since the years of the Civil War. The bloody character of this revolution was tragically revealed two weeks ago tonight in Oxford, Mississippi, when two men were killed and seventy-five were wounded in the riot that followed the admission of James Meredith to the campus of Ole Miss. You and I were not there. We did not violently defy the court order. We did not hurl stones at the marshals. We did not yell obscenities at the man. We did nothing. We did nothing about the revolution at Ole Miss. We have done nothing about the revolution here. Nothing. We live in the midst of the greatest social revolution in a century. And as a church—as a congregation of the people of God in Danville, Kentucky—we have done nothing at all. Is not this—our failure as a church to do anything at all about securing the rights of every person in our community, regardless of his race—is not this failure a sin and transgression against which the Lord God Almighty, by his very nature as God, must protest?

We mean well. We are men and women of good will. There is not a person here this morning who rejoiced over the rioting in Mississippi or who takes pride in the shedding of blood. On the contrary, we are ashamed as Christians, as Americans, as those who love the South, over what happened there. But what have we done about it? What has First Church done—not in Oxford, Mississippi, but in Danville, Kentucky—to bring healing and reconciliation among men?

There are, I know, many individuals in this church who have a social conscience informed by our Lord Jesus Christ. These persons are ready and willing to accept criticism, economic loss, personal defeat, for the sake of God's Kingdom and his righteousness; and in the affairs of daily life they serve their Lord well. But what have we done together as a church—as this particular congregation set by God in this particular community—to be his instrument of reconciliation and healing among men?

God protested against the worship of the people of ancient Israel because despite their sincerity and good intentions they ignored the plight of the needy. What must he say today?

But we have in our text not only a word of *protest* but also a word of *proclamation*. God not only tells his people what is wrong. He also tells them what is right. He not only rejects the worship they offer but also specifies the worship he wants. God is a gracious God. He does not beat his people over the head with their sins, leaving them ignorant of his will for them. No, he clarifies for them in love and mercy just what he wants them to do.

"Is not this the fast that I choose:
  to loose the bonds of wickedness,
  to undo the thongs of the yoke,
to let the oppressed go free,
  and to break every yoke?
Is it not to share your bread with the hungry,
  and bring the homeless poor into your house;
when you see the naked, to cover him,
    and not to turn your back on your fellow man?" (see Isaiah 58:6-7).

Now, there are many things in the Bible that I do not understand. I do not know how John the Baptist recognized Jesus. I do not know what to make of the demonic spirits that possessed ancient men. I do not know how to interpret some of the miracles of the Bible. Many parts of Paul's theology leave me confused. But this essential proclamation of the Lord is so clear that, try though I may, I cannot escape it. I can disregard it—and I do disregard it. I can disobey it—and I do disobey it. I can wish that it were not so—and I do wish, time and time again, that it were not so. But I cannot deny it or escape it; for I know, deep in my heart, that it is there, and that it is true and right. And in this essential proclamation God tells me that he has so identified himself with my neighbor that when I neglect or exploit or betray or turn my back on my neighbor, I am in that very same moment neglecting, exploiting, betraying, or turning my back on God.

Is not this word a call of God for us to *do* something as a congregation of his people? Is not this a divine demand that we take responsible action? God knows the problem is difficult! But can't we do something? Can't we at least publicly declare that we know, and rejoice in the fact, that God intends for his church to be a house of prayer for *all* peoples? Can't we at least try to find some way in which we can come to know our Negro neighbors here in Danville, to learn from them what it means to be a second-class citizen in our town? Can't we at least protest against the most flagrant violations of human dignity in our midst?

As many of you know, I am chairman of the Council on Christian Action for our synod. There are three Negroes on the twelve-man council. Not long ago I wanted to have an overnight meeting of the council here in Danville. I called each of our three motels to see if I could get accommodations. I laid the request on thick! I told each person who I was, who the Negroes were (a college president, a Presbyterian minister, and the minister's wife), and what the meeting was all about. The manager of one motel said he would like to accommodate us, but was afraid to. If his were the only motel accommodating Negroes, he might lose business. The clerk at the second motel told me that, the owner being out of town, he could not make the decision. The manager of the third motel was insulted that I asked her to accommodate Negroes, but she could give me rooms for the eight whites!

> "Is not this the fast that I choose:
>     to loose the bonds of wickedness,
>     to undo the thongs of the yoke,
> to let the oppressed go free,
>     and to break every yoke?"

We have in this ancient Word of God to his people a *protest,* a *proclamation,* and, finally, a *promise* of the Lord.

> "If you take away from the midst of you the yoke,
>     the pointing of the finger, and speaking wickedness,
> if you pour yourself out for the hungry
>     and satisfy the desire of the afflicted,
> then shall your light rise in the darkness
>     and your gloom be as the noonday.
> And the LORD will guide you continually,
>     and satisfy your desire with good things . . .
> And your ancient ruins shall be rebuilt;
>     you shall raise up the foundations of many generations;
> you shall be called the repairer of the breach,
>     the restorer of streets to dwell in" (Isaiah 58:9-12).

Such is the promise of the Lord. This promise of God to the people who obey him is not a guarantee of peace and prosperity, of comfort and success. We need in all honesty to recognize that if we took our Lord's proclamation seriously and tried to be faithful, if we determined as a congregation to become a house of prayer for all peoples, if we obeyed our Lord's commandment to break every yoke, we would doubtlessly be criticized and abused, and our church might well suffer both numerical and financial loss.

But God does promise to those who obey him his presence in their midst, his light for their guidance, and his glory as their refuge and strength. If you obey him, "then you shall call, and the LORD will answer; you shall cry, and he will say, Here I am" (Isaiah 58:9). This is God's word of promise, and many a church in history, suffering from persecution for righteousness' sake, has found God to be as good as his word.

# No Back Doors in Heaven

Richard S. Watt
Tabor and Harmony Presbyterian Churches
Harmony, North Carolina
June 16, 1963

Harmony is an incorporated village of five hundred persons in Piedmont North Carolina. There is little local industry besides a garment manufacturing plant and the textile mills of nearby Turnersburg and Statesville.

The Negro community is situated primarily at the edge of town and on nearby farms. Courtesy and friendliness, with segregation, have for long been the accepted interracial pattern—outwardly the town lives up to its name. Until the fall of 1964 the only threat of local interracial change was the work of some Harmony Negroes in the Statesville chapter of the NAACP. That fall, however, a few Negro students transferred to the previously white high school.

"The community appears out of the mainstream of the racial crisis," says Mr. Watt. "In Statesville the atmosphere has been more tense, focusing on the attempted desegregation of municipal swimming pools; but this situation is reflected in the thinking of communities such as Harmony. The attitude of white residents is generally one of bowing to the inevitable, while wondering 'why the Negroes keep wanting more when we have given them so much.' "

Mr. Watt became pastor of the Harmony and Tabor churches in June, 1962, immediately after graduation from seminary. The Tabor church, with forty members, is situated on a country road two miles from Harmony, while the Harmony church, with fifty members, is on the main highway which runs through town. The membership of both churches is a cross section of the community—farmers, factory workers, retired people, and a few professionals.

The sermon below was preached to both congregations at the height of the protest demonstrations which swept almost all major cities in North Carolina from April through August of 1963. "After I had already determined to preach it," says Mr. Watt, "I spent an evening with a Negro couple in Greensboro, both of whom had been actively involved in recent demonstrations there. To my question, 'When do you think pressure for desegregation will come to smaller communities like Harmony?' they replied, 'Any day.' I went home hoping to awaken the congregation to the fact and nature of the crisis, and to foster a thoughtful Christian atmosphere in advance of any specific local crisis. The sermon was received quietly, without any overt hostility. I do not think that any minds were changed, but during some subsequent visits two or three families wanted to talk about the subject. With them, at least, communication had not been cut off. The same morning I preached the sermon I asked each session to record a policy for or against admitting Negroes to worship. The Tabor Session immediately voted 'yes,' but the Harmony Session declined to take any action. By the end of 1964 there had been no testing of the policy."

TEXT: EPHESIANS 2:11-22

In the past few months history has moved so fast that we here in this small community face the possibility that what has happened in our larger cities—Birmingham and Raleigh and Durham and Greensboro—may well happen here, tomorrow or next week. Negroes who have sought the dignity of equal treatment in motels and restaurants in our large cities will sooner or later come to the Harmony Cafe and the motel here. Negroes who have sought to worship in fellowship with white Christians may come to our church doors next week—perhaps even today. I would be neglecting my duty to you if I did not try to shed the light of God's Word on the crisis that may be coming to us.

There are many reasons why we as Christians can no longer shut our eyes to the issues of race relations and desegregation. For one thing, whether we like it or not, for better or worse, the dropping of barriers between the races is inevitable. History is moving in a certain direction and it will not be turned back. Eric Sevareid, the newspaper columnist, has called the Negroes' movement a "true popular revolution" like the revolution that freed our country from Britain. This new revolution may become a war of race against race—but it need not. For its true nature, like that of those before it, is a fight for the dignity of all men equally, against those who would reserve human dignity to a privileged class— and thereby lose it, even for themselves.

Again, desegregation of the races is best for our nation, economically and politically. Equal opportunity in schooling and in employment will make more efficient use of the tremendous reservoir of talent that lies buried in the Negro, and it will raise the standard of living—and of life—for all of us.

Around the world, the United States claims to be the supporter of freedom and the leader of the free world. We can keep the confidence of the rising new nations of the world—colored nations—only as we show them that here at home we are for equal opportunity. Segregationists have made a great point of totalling the millions spent in Oxford, Mississippi, to place one Negro in the university. But the truth is that, so far as the colored nations of the world are concerned, by spending those millions our nation has put its money where its mouth is; we have shown how far we are willing to go to guarantee the right of a single individual, and that is a point in our favor in the fight for freedom.

Again, the desegregation of the races is in accord with the letter and spirit of the United States Constitution, and it will come about by law if it does not come voluntarily. Some say, "But you cannot change the hearts of men through courts or legislatures." And that is perfectly true. But murder, theft, adultery, and perjury—these are moral matters, matters of the heart. They are the subject of the Ten Commandments, and they find their place in the teaching of Jesus. None of us would want to remove from the books our laws against murder, theft, adultery, or perjury, even though these laws have no power to make men good. Just so, even if the only real solution to the race problem lies in renewing the hearts of men, still we must have laws to prevent the injustice in men's hearts from being put into practice. As Christians, we have a duty not only to seek the reforming of men's hearts, but also to protect our neighbor from murder, theft, adultery, or perjury—or injustice based on race.

But all these reasons fall short of being truly Christian reasons. What we think about race problems or anything else cannot be determined by a merely negative attitude of resignation to what is inevitable. We cannot be guided only by the selfish aim of seeking what is good for *our* country and its reputation in the world. We cannot even be governed solely by the high ideals of a great Constitution and a body of laws.

What we think and what we say and do are rooted in one thing only: the Good News of what God has done for us in Jesus Christ. We are the people to whom he has come. "God was in Christ reconciling the world to himself" (2 Corinthians 5:19). And not only to himself, but God in Christ has reconciled man to every other man. As Paul says, "He is our peace, who has made us both one, and has broken down the dividing wall of hostility . . . that he might create in himself one new man in place of the two, so making peace . . ." (Ephesians 2:14-15). Where do we find that peace? Where does that "one new man" live of whom Paul speaks? Above all, he lives in the church—the fellowship of forgiven people.

So it must be in the church—where Christians profess to seek the will of God, to hear his Word and to do it—where we receive his command to love one another, our neighbor even as ourselves —and where we try to make that command a part of our lives— here, in the church, of all places, we should be ready to repent the sins that divide race from race, man from man, and seek by God's grace to heal those divisions.

And yet the Protestant church has not been foremost, but hindmost, in healing the sin of white supremacy and segregation. The church should be the spearhead of the gospel—but it has become the rubber stamp of the culture in which it lives. In the church we now find ourselves trailing behind the secular world—lawyers, legislators, businessmen—instead of providing leadership.

Though there are many areas in the secular world where the problems of integration are complex, there is one place where *every* Christian has the answer, where even the questions disappear. That place is the church. Within the walls of the church, before the Lord's Table, all differences of intellectual ability, of class, of background, of likes and dislikes, disappear before the one fact: that we are all sinners, and we are all the beneficiaries of the grace of one Savior.

None of us comes into this sanctuary by any right of his own. All of us come as undeserving guests before this table; even as guests we are not equals with our Host, but we are like beggars invited by a rich man to share his table. We are charity cases.

This very building is God's, not ours. We have said so in dedicating it as a church building. Into this building we come as guests, and as guests we sit before his table and partake of the bread of life. If I were a guest in your home, sitting at your table, could I feel free to say to you, "Now, see here—I don't want you to invite John Doe; I'd rather not sit with him"? Would not that be the crudest kind of discourtesy—downright ingratitude to you as my host? Then as a guest in the house of God, you will not turn away another man whom *God* invites here.

But the question arises: What of the Negro who comes to church not really in response to God's invitation, not really to worship, but only to make publicity, only to test us? Professor Ben L. Rose has replied to that question in these words:

> . . . Let the church use such tests as opportunities to witness in the Spirit of Christ to the truth that God is no respecter of persons, and that in God's house and family there is no distinction between the races.
>
> On the other hand, suppose one of those Negroes who come to our church is not trying to test us, but comes in answer to the invitation of Christ. Suppose he comes athirst for the water of life, needing and seeking the Savior. And suppose we offend such a one, and turn him away! We shall answer for it in the Day of Judgment![1]

Search your own heart. Have *you* never entered the sanctuary with motives that were less than Christian? Perhaps you have come only because the neighbors would talk if you didn't show up, or because you happened to have a new hat to show off. Have you never come to worship bearing a grudge against a neighbor? We don't question the motives of our white neighbors who come here to worship. No more should we question the motives of the Negro visitor.

Suppose he does come to test us or to make publicity. It would not be the first time that outsiders have sought to test the church or to use it. Suppose our Christian witness in making him welcome among us should be the channel by which the Holy Spirit could work in his heart! Suppose that he who entered in defiance leaves in a spirit of true worship!

Let me close with a story. Some years ago a South Carolinian, whose racial views were like those of his neighbors, was approached by an elderly Negro. "Mr. Bagnal, I knew your grandmother when I was little. She was the kindest lady I ever knew, and when I'd go to her back door she'd always have a cookie for me. When I reach heaven, she is the first person I want to see. But—do you think I'll have to go to her back door?" Mr. Bagnal thought a moment and replied, "No, I'm sure there are no back doors in heaven."

"No back doors in heaven"—because heaven is where God's will is done. When we pray, "Thy will be done on *earth,* as it is in heaven," it will be a lie, unless we dedicate ourselves to end our back doors on earth.

# *Foundations*

J. Will Ormond
Covenant Presbyterian Church, Tuscaloosa, Alabama
January 12, 1964

Now a famous city in the Civil Rights struggle, Tuscaloosa has experienced a long series of crises, beginning with the 1955 riots on the University of Alabama campus in connection with the registration of Autherine Lucy. In spite of the fact that the Grand Dragon of the state's Ku Klux Klan has his headquarters in the city and in spite of Governor George Wallace's "standing in the schoolhouse door" in June of 1963, the city's business, university, and law-enforcement officials have been credited with more progress in desegregation than is characteristic of many other Alabama cities.

Thirty percent of Tuscaloosa's population of 65,000 is Negro. In late 1962 an organized protest movement (Tuscaloosa Citizens for Action) got under way in the Negro community in opposition to seating policies of the local bus company, which eventually went out of business. But by 1964 most public facilities were known to be desegregated; voting privileges for the Negro community were legally uncontested; ten Negro students were studying at the university; and one white student was enrolled at all-Negro Stillman College. At the end of this decade of developments, many local leaders felt that only two areas of community life were still major resistance-points to the movement toward institutional desegregation: employment and the church.

For many years, the very presence of Stillman College, founded in 1876 by southern Presbyterians concerned for the cause of higher education among Negroes, has exerted gentle pressure toward the desegregation of local church meetings. The pressure has mounted in recent years as a growing number of Stillman's six hundred students have become involved in civil rights activity.

50

The Covenant Presbyterian Church is one of three southern Presbyterian congregations in the city.[1] Organized in 1949 to serve one of the city's growing suburban areas, the congregation now numbers about four hundred persons, a large proportion of whom are identified with the business and professional communities, the university, and the white contingent of the Stillman faculty.

The following sermon was preached on an occasion when a member of the Negro contingent of that faculty was present at the Sunday morning worship of the Covenant Church, accompanied by his family and two Stillman students. It is the only sermon in this collection which does not mention the words "race" or "segregation"; but it is unmistakably related to the meaning of these words in the churches of central Alabama. "During the fifteen years of my pastorate (1949-64)," says southern-born Will Ormond, "I rarely preached a sermon which spoke solely and specifically to the racial situation. I mentioned the issue often enough, however, to cause some persons in the congregation to believe that I harped on it continually. Over the years the congregation has experienced some steady growth towards maturity in the matter, but we have had our times of testing. One must live in this area to know the electric and bitter tension that the slightest deviation from the racial *status quo* can produce."

This particular sermon was actually preached twice, once in relation to this congregation's wrestle with the issue of racial inclusiveness and a second time (four months later) in relation to that same struggle on the floor of Tuscaloosa Presbytery. "The first occasion," says Mr. Ormond, "was a time of considerable tension in the congregation. Many months before, by a slim majority, the session had passed a resolution establishing a closed-door policy. Then, only a few weeks before the preaching of this sermon, still by a slim majority, the session had reversed that resolution, establishing an open-door policy. The action caused immediate unrest and dissatisfaction among some sections of the congregation. A few members withheld or reduced their financial support; others absented themselves from worship or from their accustomed duties. The sermon was prepared with these things in mind and specifically in relation to the fact that, at the end of the worship service of January 12, we were to ordain and install a newly elected group of deacons. The sermon was prepared without the knowledge that the students and faculty family from Stillman would be with us, but the meaning of the sermon for their presence was evident to almost everyone. Said one member to me afterwards, 'I think that was probably the best sermon you ever preached yesterday, but I couldn't hear it.' Many people in the congregation were sympathetic to the session's new policy, however, and the policy is still standing. I believe that the membership as a whole has come through the crisis remarkably well."

On the second occasion, when the sermon was delivered in slightly revised form, Tuscaloosa Presbytery was faced with the question of receiving into its organizational bounds three Negro Presbyterian congregations which were already within its geographical bounds.[2] Two weeks before, the 1964 General Assembly had "instructed" its presbyteries to take steps to eliminate the so-called Negro presbyteries in the denomination and "to begin this process promptly";[3] and the Synod of Alabama, meeting the previous year, had also requested its presbyteries to consider this action. "I had been asked to preach the sermon of the morning at this meeting of presbytery," reports Mr. Ormond. "A committee of presbytery, of which I was a member, had been studying the issue for some time, and a negative majority report was to be brought in that very morning. A minority report, signed by one other minister and myself, was also to be presented. In the sermon I tried to speak the same word to presbytery that I had tried to speak to the Covenant congregation four months before. But the vote was disappointing this time. Over the signed protest of thirteen ministers, presbytery refused to abide by the instruction of the General Assembly."

Theologically considered, says Mr. Ormond, "the church is not a democracy." But humanly considered, the church which he addresses is a democracy. Caught at this ambiguous crossing, all five sermons of this opening section have shared a common agony.

## TEXT: 1 CORINTHIANS 12:1-7, 12-21, 24-27

We are met today as a congregation of the Presbyterian Church in the United States. We are members of a denomination committed to certain doctrines and principles. Presbyterians believe that the growth, the effectiveness, and the health of the church depend in large measure upon how well we understand and how surely we live up to these doctrines.

The doctrines of our church are not exclusively Presbyterian, but each one is emphasized and stressed in our creed, and from time to time we need to consider the foundations of that creed.

I would call your attention to three such foundations—the three primary ones.

The first of these is the Lordship of Jesus Christ. The very earliest Christian creed was "Jesus is Lord," and all the rest of theology is commentary on that brief declaration. Paul wrote, "No one can say 'Jesus is Lord' except by the Holy Spirit." For one to recognize the Lordship of Jesus Christ takes an act of God in the heart of a man.

What do we mean when we say that Jesus Christ is Lord? We mean that he rules, that he is over all, that he directs, that he is sovereign, that to him belong our sole and highest loyalty and allegiance.

Why is he Lord? He is Lord because of who he is in his person. Jesus Christ is one with us; he is human as we are human; he has identified himself with men and understands us from within our humanity. But the very miracle of his humanness is the fact that he is the Word made flesh. Perhaps it is easy for us to picture Jesus in long flowing robes and walking along the picturesque lanes of Galilee as he pats little children on the head and speaks gently of peace and love. But it is not quite so easy for us to see him as the first chapter of Revelation portrays him—a dazzling, awesome figure with eyes like flames of fire, feet like burnished bronze, his voice like the sound of many waters, a sharp two-edged sword issuing from his mouth, and in his hand the seven stars symbolizing the universal church. It is difficult for us to grasp those passages of Scripture which say of him, "He is the image of the invisible God," "in him all things were created," "He is before all things, and in him all things hold together," "in him all the fulness of God was pleased to dwell" (Colossians 1: 15-17, 19).

This Jesus Christ is not one who is so much like us that we can transfer our feelings, our prejudices, our notions, to our own image of him. We like to feel that because *we* think in such and such a manner, Jesus, our human friend, feels exactly the same way about it. No, this one who has revealed himself in human flesh is the Lord of heaven and earth, and before him we bow in awe and worship and submission. We do not say to him, "Jesus, my dear friend, I would that thou wouldst do for me whatsoever I desire." Rather it is our part to fall down before the blinding light of his majesty and cry, "Lord, what wouldst thou have me to do?"

Jesus Christ is Lord also because of what he has done. He emptied himself, he gave himself, he did not count equality with God a thing to be grasped. But he took upon himself the form of a servant. He suffered unto death. He purchased the church with his own blood—that is, with the complete giving of his life. He did not purchase the church with a few hours of his time after he had taken care of all his own interests. He did not purchase the church with the giving of some of the surplus of his means. He purchased the church with his own blood. Therefore, the church is his and he is the head of it. We are easily prone to speak of "my church" or "our church" and to assert our proprietorship over it because of what we have given to it or done for it or because of some inherited connection with it. But none has a right to call the church "mine" except the one who purchased it with his own blood. God himself recognized Jesus' giving of his life, for he raised him from the dead and gave him all authority and all power and made him the head of the church.

Now what does this Lordship of Christ mean for the church? It means that the church is responsible first of all to Christ, the head of the church. It means that the church determines its decisions not by what it believes to be the desire of a majority of its members nor by the prevailing atmosphere and custom of the time. It means that the officers and members ask about every action: "Is this action being taken under conscious submission to the Lordship of Christ and solely in accordance with his will?"

This question, brethren, is not an easy one to answer. It almost always involves struggle and the surrender of some of our own cherished desires and preferences. This may sound un-American, but the church is not a democracy. The gospel is not decided by majority vote. The church is a theocracy. It is totalitarian in its rulership. For Christ is its sovereign; he is its absolute authority. Only insofar as the church is ruled by Jesus Christ, its head, is it truly the church. He rules in the church insofar as the congregation in its corporate life and individual members in their daily relationships submit to the Lordship of Christ.

It is an easy thing to say that we recognize his Lordship, but it is not an easy thing to live by. Far too often we get around it in some such fashion as this: "I am a Christian. I have accepted Christ as personal Lord and Savior. I am even an officer in the church. Therefore, what I think is right is his will. What makes me feel good is Christian. What goes against the grain and disturbs me is wrong." But this is not surrender to Christ; this is calling upon Christ to surrender to us. To submit to the Lordship of Christ calls for struggle and prayer and the agonizing releasing of our own wills to the will of God. Even Jesus himself had to go through the ordeal of the Garden of Gethsemane as he searched for the will of his Father and sought to bring his own will into conformity with the will of God. If this is the path our Lord had to take, should we hope for a painless and effortless molding of our stubborn wills to the will of God?

But how are we to know the will of the Lord? This leads us to the second foundation, and that is the authority of Scripture. Christians are the people of the Book. We believe that the Holy Spirit inspired men of old to write the Scriptures and that through them he spoke. But we also believe that the Holy Spirit is eternal and active and that therefore he can and does still speak through these same documents which he caused to be written so long ago. The very first chapter of the Westminster Confession of Faith is, "Of the Holy Scripture." The first question put to church officers upon ordination is, "Do you believe the Scriptures of the Old and New Testaments to be the Word of God, the only infallible rule of faith and practice?" When a man answers that question in the affirmative he means that he accepts the Scriptures as his guide and authority. He means that where the Scriptures speak he will listen, he will act, he will obey. He means that he will always be open for new light to break from God's Word. He means that he will not be guided by his own opinion, his own preferences, nor by the pressures of circumstances, traditions, or groups, but only by the Word of God. Many times we piously state that we follow our conscience in the decisions that we make, but conscience is a poor guide unless we can say as did Luther, "My conscience is captive to the Word of God."

If we are to recognize the authority of Scripture and take the Word of God as our guide, then it follows that we must know what that Word is. We must not be content with a casual reading of a verse here and there, but we must come to this Word diligently and with open minds and hearts, asking God to speak to us through it. We must not come with minds already made up as to what the Word ought to say or as to what we would like for it to say. Rather, we must come ready to hear what it does say whether we like it or not. Too often we search the Scriptures looking for props for our prejudices. Too often we force the Word to speak our words rather than letting it, under the Holy Spirit's power, speak God's.

It is a dangerous thing to discover what God's Word really says. For once we have discovered it, we are under obligation both by reason of our relationship to Christ and by the vows we have taken as church officers to obey that Word.

The Lordship of Christ and the authority of Scripture lead us to the third foundation, and that is the unity of the church. If Jesus Christ is Lord, then he is the head of the church, and the church can have only one head. If the church has one head, then it is one body and all members are united one to the other. If we are members of his body, then, whether we like it or not, we are united inevitably to all other members of that body. We are united to our fellow Christians, whoever and wherever they are, not because they all look like us, not because they all think our thoughts, not because we are naturally congenial with them all, not because we all have the same background and culture. We are united to our fellow Christians solely because all of us are united to Christ, the head of the church.

The authority of Scripture also leads us to the unity of the church. What is the Bible all about? It is the record of God's mighty acts. It is the record of what God has been doing all through history. And what has he been doing? God has been calling to himself a people—a people for his purpose. This is what he was doing when he called Abraham, when he called

Israel, and this is what he is doing now as he calls us—his church —to be the instrument of his purpose in the world. He is calling a people to be the instrument of his purpose of reconciliation in this divided world. He is calling that people—his church—to demonstrate in their own corporate life that unity which comes from being reconciled to God and to one another.

Our Presbyterian constitution defines the visible church as consisting of "all those who make profession of their faith in the Lord Jesus Christ, together with their children."[4] The church is a colony of heaven set in a pagan world. It is not an earthly club for spiritual aristocrats.

If we are members of the Presbyterian Church in Tuscaloosa, or Eutaw, or Selma, or Linden, then we are members of the Presbyterian Church in the whole United States. And if we are members of the Presbyterian Church, then we are members of the church universal. We cannot put restrictions or limitations of our own choosing upon our membership, for we are members one of another.

The Lordship of Christ, the authority of Scripture, the unity of the church—brethren, these are the foundations of Presbyterian doctrine and polity. May we take our stand upon these foundations and never forsake them.

# *Not Race But Grace*

Robert H. Walkup
First Presbyterian Church, Starkville, Mississippi
September 30-October 7, 1962

In the midst of a culture which for long has emphasized the virtues of social harmony, how does the Presbyterian make theological response to the onset of social disorder? The next seven contributions, three of them from one minister, are some answers to this question.

Starkville, Mississippi, is the county seat of Oktibbeha County, in the east central part of the state. The population of the town is some 15,000, of whom about one fourth are Negro. The county is dairy country, but the commanding industry of the town is the state's five-thousand-student land-grant university—Mississippi State. As a university town, Starkville has a sizable number of residents from other parts of the nation; and, especially in the three large downtown churches (Baptist, Methodist, Presbyterian), this variety of backgrounds helps to create some openness to the challenge of deep-South traditions.

Many of the wage earners among Starkville's Negroes are employees of the university. They hold the best jobs open to Negroes in the county, but are constantly subject to control through intimidation. One evidence of this has been the lack of militancy in the recent history of the town's race relations. If James Meredith had decided to be an engineer rather than a lawyer, however, the name Starkville might have been as internationally known today as is Oxford, one hundred miles to the north.

Robert H. Walkup became pastor of the First Presbyterian Church of Starkville in 1953, after making clear to the officers of the church that he had "a very tender conscience on the race question." From this beginning and repeatedly in his preaching over a decade, says he, "the congregation had little difficulty knowing my views on that or any other question. And they must have recognized me as a person who wanted to be a pastor as well as a prophet. By 1962 I had been with most of them in sorrow and in joy. They called me at all times and for just about everything. I told them often that they were my sheep and that I was grateful that God had called me to serve Him by serving them. To this they responded."

The members of the congregation responded so well that in the summer of 1963 the elders ventured the decision to open the church's doors to any person who came to worship, with the qualification that no church member would be subject involuntarily to sharing a pew with a Negro visitor. In the following week, however, pressure for a reversal of this policy was put upon the elders by local and statewide leaders, most of them outside the congregation. At a meeting the next Sunday, for the sake of church unity a majority of the session voted for the reversal, against a persisting minority of four. A unanimous vote of confidence in Dr. Walkup accompanied this action.

A year later, after eleven years in Starkville, Dr. Walkup accepted a call to the First Presbyterian Church of McAllen, Texas. "The decision was very difficult. Recent disturbances in the Synod of Mississippi, in which I had been heavily involved; the distress I felt over the policy of barring the door to some of God's people; and the tug of the call to McAllen had to be weighed over against the continued mutual affection between the Starkville congregation and myself."

Describing his ministry during the Oxford crisis, Dr. Walkup comments that "all the people could see well enough that it just as easily could have been us. That is the main reason I kept coming back to the matter in my preaching. In addition to this I called on businessmen and tried to tell them that a riot could destroy our community. In the state as a whole there was the feeling that 'old Ross' [Governor Barnett] could outfox the Kennedy boys and that Mississippi would win. Some of the talk and some of the deals were close to treason. I said again and again that I was not a Mississippian who happened to be in America but an American who happened to be in Mississippi.

"All these sermons were taped and broadcast at 12:30 each Sunday. Many Negroes heard them, for they often told me so, and sometimes they thanked me for them. During this time it was a widely shared opinion that the ministry would be wise to be silent. One nearby Pres-

byterian minister preached a sermon thanking God for men of courage like St. Paul and Governor Barnett. At the mid-October meeting
of St. Andrews Presbytery, I was an active supporter of the successful
move of Presbytery to send out a pastoral letter to all its churches
urging Presbyterians to stand for law and order. The sermons plus the
Presbytery action raised some resistance in my own congregation, yet
nobody left the church. One lady called to ask me not to preach again
on the Ole Miss situation. She asked if I had lost faith in them. I told
her that I had not, and more than that I had not quit loving them. She
replied, 'Well, then, you preach whatever you want to preach.' "

The first sermon below was preached on Sunday morning, September 30. For some days before, state officials had been announcing
their intention to defy the ruling of the Federal Circuit Court of Ap-
peals requiring the admittance of James Meredith to the university.
That night rioting broke out in Oxford, killing two persons. It was one
week before World-Wide Communion Sunday.

## TEXT: JAMES 1:1-8

These are difficult days. You know that without my telling you.
You know how we've lived these last hours—prisoners of the
news reports—hearing what we could hear and reading what we
could read, and all of it seeming to us almost like a nightmare, a
disquieting dream from some fantastic place unknown. And yet
we've known in our hearts all along, that were it not for God's
own mercy, what is happening a hundred miles away could just as
well be happening right here. And we're involved! As a minister
of Jesus Christ—indeed, as just a common garden-variety Christian—I'm troubled!

There is a word of Scripture which keeps haunting me: "What
do ye more than others?" *We are Christians!* We are not politicians. We are not skilled to understand maneuvering—but we
are Christians! For two thousand years now the gospel has been
saturating our thoughts. Do we know any more than the others
know? Is there any contribution that we can make that non-
Christians cannot make? "What do ye *more* than others?"

Will you hear the text? "If any of you lack wisdom, let him ask
of God, that giveth to all men liberally, and upbraideth not; and it
shall be given him. But let him ask in faith, nothing doubting."[1]

You remember that our good friend Martin Luther didn't care much for the Epistle of St. James. Martin Luther, who was given sometimes to extravagance of language, referred to the Epistle of James as an epistle of straw. You see, Martin Luther couldn't use the Epistle of James for what he was trying to do. He was in an argument, and while he was in an argument he was looking for what weapons he could find, and the Epistle of James didn't have any weapons. It's not a theological epistle. If you want theology, go to Romans. So Luther went to Romans. But what James is trying to do is just deal with the everyday problems of Christian living. He seldom touches any of the deep, profound, involved truths. Even so, he can speak to us; even so, he has a word we need today—or at least a word that helps me. Let's look at that text: "If any of you lack wisdom . . ."

Now wasn't that a courteous way for James to put it? Wasn't that nice of James to put that "if" in there? Was there really any doubt in his mind about whether or not we lack wisdom? Wisdom to James did not mean learning or profundity of thought but the ability to use the trials of life—the ability to discern in life itself the will of God. Now, do we lack that? For all of our supposed learning . . . for all of our big talk . . . do we lack wisdom? There is no hope really for us as long as we think that we're wise. As long as we keep on believing that wisdom was born with us and that understanding shall perish with our going. Only men who confuse themselves with God will dare to pretend in this anguished and troubled day that they know the exact route to the Promised Land. Only men who take unto themselves the omnipotence that belongs to the Lord God Almighty alone will believe that they have in their own mind this day every answer and every truth.

Only Job's comforters will offer us now shallow answers to these questions. Do we lack wisdom? *Certainly* we lack wisdom! We've got cleverness in abundance, but cleverness is not what the Scripture's talking about—and it's not what we need. We need wisdom, and hope begins with our knowing that we need it! There is hope for us only if we realize that we don't possess wisdom. Only if we realize that we are desperately in need. "If any of you lack wisdom," says James, "let him ask God."

But that seems too simple. If any man lacks wisdom, ask God, that's—oh—we've grown past that, haven't we? Just ask? That simple! But the New Testament certainly puts it that way, doesn't it? And the Apostles believed it. St. Paul was quite sure, you know, that he lived by prayer. St. Paul was quite sure that his missionary journeys were guided by the will of God in answer to his prayers. And did not our Divine Redeemer himself spend much time in prayer? But we've grown beyond that, haven't we . . . or have we?

Do we really think we'll get wisdom these days by *sharing our common ignorance?* By pooling our misinformation? Or do we think, perchance, we'll get wisdom by asking God? That's the lesson of history that we have to relearn again, and again, and again; and we don't want to ask God. Sometimes we're afraid to ask God.

You will remember that one time there was an assembly of supposedly large men in Westminster Abbey. You will remember that the great bulk of these men were Englishmen—and the seasoning of the group was Scottish. They had met together to write a statement of Christian belief, which later became the Westminster Confession of Faith and the Larger and Shorter Catechisms. But this assembly was split, and there was in that assembly almost the most learned man in Christendom, a Dr. John Selden. He was the great champion of the Erastian heresy. You all know the Erastian heresy, you just don't know it by that name. That's the heresy which teaches the supremacy of the state over the church. It's still with us. And Dr. Selden, learnedly and persuasively, presented the position of the Erastians in the assembly. And the poor Presbyterians had about given up hope. They felt that what he said was heresy, but they didn't know where to grab it to grapple with it. A saintly young Scotsman, almost the youngest man there, named George Gillespie, got up to speak. They'd watched him while Dr. Selden was speaking and all the time he'd been writing on a pad before him. He got up and put his hand on that pad and began to speak. And he spoke for an hour! Dr. Selden, himself, said later that in that one hour George Gillespie destroyed ten years of study and work for him. And the whole course of that assembly was changed. So men rushed to that note pad. They wanted to see his notes—the outline from which he had spoken. And over and over again he'd written on that pad one Latin phrase: "Da lucem, Domine"—"Give light, O Lord."[2]

"Give light, O Lord"—that could be our prayer. We could spend the rest of this Lord's Day praying—for wisdom—for light —for understanding! We need light today, not heat. What we need today is not men with hot heads and big mouths, but men with cool heads and warm hearts. We've talked on the street corners now to about everybody, haven't we? How much have we talked in the closet to God? We've talked about men—but have we talked to *God* about them? We have a solemn duty of prayer. "If any of you lack wisdom, let him ask of God." We've gathered our neighbors' opinions, but have we asked God's? He says, "But ask in faith, nothing doubting"—that's the condition. He promises wisdom if we ask for it, provided we ask in faith, nothing doubting. "Nothing 'wavering,'" the Greek really says. For God will do nothing for a double-minded man who says, "Yes," and then again, "No"; nor for a man who says, "I trust in God, but I trust in myself too." We must come dependent, wholly and completely dependent upon God's wisdom, God's mercy, God's providence.

Now listen to me carefully, because you're not going to like what I say, some of you! (That's all right. I've said it to God and I've already talked this sermon over with God. He likes it.)

*I don't believe in state sovereignty!*
*I don't believe in national sovereignty!*

All this talk about the United States government being sovereign is *foolishness!* And all this talk about the State of Mississippi being sovereign is *foolishness!* Sovereign means: "one who has power that is not diminished by anything anywhere." There is only one type of sovereignty and that's absolute sovereignty, *and that belongs to God!* And that's the *only* place it belongs. If we lack wisdom, if we lack understanding, if we are troubled in this day, we will turn back where we should have been, God pity us, all along—to the one who really owns us, to the one whose world this *really* is.

I read somewhere that Wendell Phillips frequently got discouraged. When he came home one day there was a large black wreath on the door. And when he came in, all the shades were drawn, and there was black all over the house. When his mother came to meet him, she was dressed in black and wearing a veil. He ran to her and said, "Mother! Who's dead?" And she said, "God." He thought she'd lost her mind; he called to her and said, "What did you say?" And she replied, "I said God is dead! I know he must be dead, because you've lost hope and as long as he's alive there's no reason to lose hope."

And now I want to give you one statement from the book of Revelation: "Alleluia: for the Lord God omnipotent reigneth."[3]

*Prayer:* We lack wisdom! We lack understanding! We're not men of good will. We have trusted in our cleverness. But now we trust in thee. Now we cry unto thee, O Lord God. Now we beg thee, O Lord God, take us and lead us through troubled days, for Jesus' sake. Amen.


*October 3, 1962.* The First Presbyterian Church of Starkville frequently had a Communion Preparation Service at the Wednesday night prayer meeting before Communion Sunday. The two murders of the previous Sunday night had now stirred all Mississippi. Automobiles on the Starkville streets had blossomed with bumper stickers saying, "Get the Castro brothers out of Washington" and "Help Ross Keep Mississippi Sovereign." Confederate flags had been unfurled in many windows. Attendance at prayer meeting that night was a little larger than usual.


TEXT: JOB 1:1-5

May God have mercy upon our souls, beloved in Jesus Christ. For now we are called to come to the table of our Lord to reach forth our bloodstained hands to receive his broken body and his shed blood. So soon after the shedding of blood in our state. May God have mercy upon us all.

We are meeting here to prepare our hearts and souls. To that end I have chosen a text: "Job said, 'It may be that my sons have sinned, and cursed God in their hearts'" (Job 1:5).

Job has become the symbol of patience, and we live in an impatient age. But what we have here is much more than the story of patience. The third chapter is not especially patient. Job was a great man—the greatest man in the East—blameless and upright. He was a loyal servant of God, a man of great wealth with farflung holdings, and the father of seven sons and three daughters. Like any modern parent, he worried about his children. He worried about his sons, and he sacrificed for them lest haply they had sinned. For as he said, "It may be that my sons have sinned, and cursed God in their hearts."

Look at this man. First, *Job was a good father*. He had genuine and deep concern for the spiritual destiny of his sons, and once a year he offered burnt offerings in their behalf. He wanted these boys to do right and he recognized their need for spiritual growth. It is good for us to notice this as we come to Holy Communion. It is good for us to see that Job, with all of his power and wealth, had time for the spiritual. The sacrament for which we prepare cannot be weighed on material scales. Like these sons of Job, we need someone who is concerned for us.

In the second place, though Job was a good man, *he made a serious mistake*. He confessed and sacrificed for his sons lest haply they had sinned. Could it be that in his concern for the sins of his sons he forgot Job and the sins of Job? For it was Job who cursed the day he was born. Now let that speak to us in this dark hour. For we, too, are quite ready to confess for others. How quickly we have confessed the sins of President Kennedy in the last few days, and how quickly we have confessed the sins of Governor Barnett. This tragedy, this shame from which we are still numb—we confess that it is the result of sin. Was it the sin of the State Highway Patrol or the U.S. marshals which caused this thing? Maybe it was the outsiders—the hoodlums and the thugs who came pouring into our state. I was in Oxford Monday of this week, and what a sight I saw! The whole square was filled with men and boys—men of hate and violence, men who had come to defy the United States Army! Very well then, is the blood on their hands? Will it help much if I confess their sins? No! The blood is on my hands! For I, together with too many of our people, helped to create the impression that we wanted them. We made way for the men of violence.

And now—now we are meeting here tonight because soon we must come to Christ's table. Soon we must receive his body which was, you remember, broken by men of violence; his blood which was, you remember, shed by men who lived by hate. Can we come to his table with hate in our hearts? Can we do this in remembrance of him while we still feel contempt for some of his brothers? Contempt for those for whom he died?

Oh, my dear ones—my poor sheep for whom God has made me an under-shepherd, what can I say to you or to me? I have wept for us all these days. I can truthfully say with the psalmist, "Tears have been my meat day and night." We talk too much and we don't say enough, then something happens. Two thousand years of the gospel of Christ! It is too late now—we, too, confess the sins of other men. *Mea culpa,* God be merciful to me a sinner! There is blood on my hands; there is blood on all our hands, and nothing can cleanse us but the grace of God.

Now, if I stopped and if I only told you that Job was a good father and that Job made a mistake, I would send you forth not only unprepared, but uncomforted. Worse still, I would send you forth without the gospel. Job sacrificed for his children, but One greater than Job has sacrificed for His children, even the sinless One. The sacrament itself speaks our words of healing and comfort. We are sinners, but we are sinners for whom Christ died. We are rebels and we have been caught with our weapons in our hands. But we are rebels whom he came to reconcile. So, in Christ's name, by the wounds of Christ, I bid you come to his table. In Christ's name, let us all cry out for forgiveness so we may be whole again. This will I do, my dying Lord—I will remember thee!

*October 7, 1962:* A week after the riot, tempers had begun to cool in Starkville. Among some citizens the defiance which had pervaded the previous seven days began to be supplanted by shame for the anarchy and notoriety which had befallen Mississippi. It was now World-Wide Communion Sunday.

TEXT: JOB 19:25; 35:1-16

When you consider the football scores, it was a great weekend for us in Starkville. But we had a weekend a week ago that wasn't a great weekend. Since we last assembled in this place something has happened that has hurt our whole state, and nation, and world. Many good weekends, but a week ago tragedy struck —and it's too familiar to need my description at this time.

I am a minister of Jesus Christ—a Presbyterian *Calvinist* minister, if you please—a child of the Reformation, a believer in the Confession of Faith, which has said always that all events alike are under the sovereign will of God; which says that God is working out his purpose in the lives and times of men.

Now, believing that, do I not find myself, and do you not find yourself, crushed down between the horns of a cruel dilemma? How can we put what has happened into line with what we know of *God?* Why? *Why?* WHY did God let this happen? Why did God let us come to this day? Look to the Bible.

I've spent some time on my knees this week. I've spent some time searching, searching again not only my heart but the Scriptures. What do they say? Well, I found my friend Job there. (Some of you were here Wednesday night and we looked at him then. Let's look at him now.) For Job had a question not unlike our question. It was the same one-word question. As we frame this word with our lips, "why," so did Job.

You remember him. He was the greatest man in the East, wealthy and upright before God. He had seven sons and three daughters, thousands of cattle and camels. And yet the day dawned when all of his sons were killed. His daughters were destroyed. His cattle were stolen and his camels were driven away. Why?

His friends came to sit with him and take counsel with him. And they sat, considerately enough, silent for a while. Then they began to say, "Job, did anything like this ever happen to an upright man?"

Then it must follow that this is punishment for sin. Now, that's not the right answer. That was not the right answer for Job, but it was a part of the answer to the problem of Job, and it's a part of the answer to our question today.

If we want to know why God let this thing come to us—if we want to know why we've been put through this day in our state— a part of the answer is . . . *sin!* A part of the answer is punishment for sin! Because the first thing I think we learn from the book of Job is that God's providence is *penal*. Or take it out of "theological" terms. Put it simply: there *is* such a thing as punishment. *Part* of the reason this has come to us is our sin.

It was a long time ago when men stole other men. It was a long time ago and very, very far away when men . . . when *men* went out to steal other men, and they brought them to our shores and they sold them in slavery.

*That was sin!*

You see, there was more to slavery than we remember. There was more to slavery than the magnolias and the mint juleps, more to slavery than the happy carefree people, more to slavery than the nice aspects of "ol' mastah" and "ol' missus" that we like to talk about. There were people being put through a wringer so severe that they cried out: "NOBODY KNOWS THE TROUBLE I'VE SEEN! NOBODY KNOWS BUT JESUS!" There were people being put through a wringer so severe that they cried out for a chariot to swing low and take them away from it.

*That was SIN!*

And we paid for that sin. We paid for it frightfully when this whole section of our nation was almost completely destroyed.

A year ago last summer I walked over the battlefields. The scars will always be on the face of Virginia and those states where the bulk of the war was fought. I walked over the battlefields, and I stopped to read at Chancellorsville and Fredericksburg and Appomattox and Manassas. I read the things they put up there on those bronze tablets. And every bit of work, every load that was lifted, every bale of cotton that was picked by the slaves, was *not worth that!*

Nothing could have been worth the carnage that swept over this nation. And our southland is not yet over it!

Now I know there are two sides. I know that more than slavery was involved. Certainly I do. If I hadn't known it, my grand-mother saw to it that I understood there was another side. But *both* sides paid, because there is such a thing as the penal provi-dence of God!

When I was a little boy in Senatobia (you know, I'm a Missis-sippian; I was surprised this week to discover somebody didn't know that—I thought I bragged about it!—but I'll tell you again), when I was a little boy in Senatobia, I came home from school one day at noon, as we did every day. After lunch we started back to school. When I got along there about where Mr. Jess French's hotel was, I saw a crowd of people watching. They were crowding into a store, so I crowded in with them. And because I was small, I wound and wiggled my way through the crowd to see what they were looking at in the store. And I saw . . . I saw a man on the floor dead! I saw a man who had been shot about five minutes. He was "black."

I asked, when I got out of that crowd, I asked who shot him, and they told me—and it nearly broke my heart. It was the man who let me ride his Shetland pony. It was the man who only a summer or two before had put his Shetland pony in our yard and left him there all summer so John and I could ride. And I went running to my grandfather distraught. And I said, "Poppa! Will they hang him?"

He said, "No, now calm down, son."

"They'll hang him, won't they, poppa?"

"No, they won't hang him."

"Well, what *will* they do to him?"

He said, "Now let that alone, boy." And so when it came out in the paper, I learned my first legal term.

"Poppa, what does n-o-l-p-r-o-s spell?"

"It spells 'nol. pros.' Why, son?"

Well, that's what they did; they nol-prossed the case. What does that mean? It means *sin,* that's what it means. It was wrong! And my grandfather was the best man I ever knew! My grandfather was better than Job—but he didn't say a word. He didn't say a *word!* He didn't do a *thing!*

I'm his grandson, and I'm paying for that sin and the sins of others who were silent, and I have four children. I'm paying because we have allowed to grow up in our hearts contempt for other men. The long years of our semi-quasi approval of lynching did something to make the climate in which we could give way to mob violence. The long years that we went through left a contempt for law and order. And that's part of our trouble today. When we think God doesn't punish us, we're not really thinking. And part of the answer to our "why" today is the punishment of God. God's providence is penal.

But God's providence, as Job found out, is also educational. God's providence does not only punish us, but it also teaches us.

I like ol' Elihu. Elihu was a young man and so he had to be silent until all the old men could talk. That must have been a terrible burden for Elihu to bear. But finally, when all the old men had talked forever and said nothing, Elihu began. In the course of his great speech he said, "But none says, '. . . God my Maker . . . gives songs in the night' " (Job 35:10).

There's more than punishment for sins. There is also *learning* to be had. Men in all ages have learned from the experiences of Job. And this speaks to us. Why? Why has God let us come to this? That we may learn a more excellent way! That we may learn from this shame and from this heartache a more excellent way.

"All they that take the sword shall perish with the sword" (Matthew 26:52, K.J.V.). It was a long time ago when our Lord Christ said that any man that calleth his brother a fool (*Raca*— one could translate it "I spit on you") is in danger of hell's fire. But we haven't learned it yet. What have we learned?

I picked up the paper and read quotations from students at Ol' Miss. And what did they say? Well, one of them said, "If I was sure I wouldn't get caught, I'd go kill that man now!" Two or three more affirmed their desire to kill somebody. Do we not know that there is in the Old Testament a *commandment against killing?* Do we not know that in the New Testament it gets *stronger?* That in the New Testament it is not only killing that is prohibited, it's the desire to kill? *Do we not know that if we have in our hearts a desire to kill someone, we have already committed murder and stand guilty before God?*

We've paid a frightful tuition for what we've learned. But wouldn't it be a dreadful thing to go through these days and not learn a thing? I pray that the good God will hasten our growth in grace. I pray that we'll know what we need to learn: *that we cannot keep on planting thistles and expecting to pick strawberries off of them!* Thistles yield thistles—and that's all they ever yield.

God's providence is educational and penal, but most of all . . . (You know I don't like to preach like this. You know what I like to preach about; what I like to preach about is the grace of God.) I'm glad we've come now to where not only can I say God's providence is penal, God's providence is educational, but God's providence is redemptive. Redemptive! The very tragedy through which Job passed brought him close to God.

He could now say, "I know that my redeemer liveth" (Job 19:25, K.J.V.). We, too, can be brought near to God.

Sin is a stubborn fact, but the cross is also a fact! The cross speaks of God's unfailing love. Here we see in spite of sin the *redemptive purpose of God.*

And now, let us repent, and now let us come to his table that we may receive the dear Sacrament of Holy Communion. Here in his broken body and shed blood God speaks the visible word: the word of reconciliation, of forgiveness, of health.

# Love Disqualified

Charles L. Stanford, Jr.
Jones Memorial Presbyterian Church, Meridian, Mississippi
October 7, 1962

With a population of 50,000, Meridian, Mississippi, is the second largest city in the state. Even prior to the riots at Oxford, business interests in the city had sought to protect the city from the disaster of "another Little Rock." Irregular gains had been made in municipal employment of Negroes, in news coverage of the Negro community, and in the willingness of some citizen groups to protest vocally the closing of public schools to save segregation. Although the segregationist mind was strongly entrenched within the city, the Citizens Council and the Ku Klux Klan had not achieved an influential status, and by 1963 the united front of segregation was visibly breached. By 1964 a Freedom School of the Council of Federated Organizations (COFO) seemed well established in the community, despite general disapproval of its aims.

Unlike the average southern Presbyterian church, the Jones Memorial Church is located in a neighborhood whose residents are largely wage earners. Its 230 members include many widowed and retired people, most of them native Mississippians. The congregation is segregated by explicit sessional policy, which provides for the possibility that a Negro wishing sincerely to worship will be permitted to do so in the basement of the church via a public address system.

Charles L. Stanford, Jr., became pastor of the congregation in 1959. Though he had made repeated references to the race issue during every year of his ministry, the Oxford riot was the occasion for this, his only sermon devoted completely to the subject. The immediate context of the sermon is best stated in his own words:

"On the Sunday prior to this sermon, at evening worship I had prayed that the forthcoming integration of the University of Mississippi would be achieved peacefully and would be accepted by all of our citizens. When I reached home that evening, I discovered that there was a full-scale riot going on at the university and that at least two people were dead.

"The next morning a prominent Baptist minister, in charge of the television devotional, preached on how to overcome the depression of a blue Monday. Later that week, the Presbyterian Ministers' Association voted down my proposal for a public statement on the Ole Miss riot. Sometime during that week I read *The Magnolia Jungle,* autobiography of P. D. East, heroic newspaper editor who was completely ostracized from his community. Then, too, I heard the remarks of the Governor calling upon the citizenry to resist integration with all means at their disposal, 'legal or otherwise.' All of these things were playing upon my mind when I wrote this sermon for the following Sunday morning.

"After the sermon had been preached, I noticed that one of the elders refused the sacrament and another hesitated before halfheartedly sipping his grape juice. Whether anyone else refused the Communion that Sunday, I do not know.

"Following evening worship that day, I happened to ride by the home of one of the elders, and seeing the familiar automobiles, realized that the session had gathered secretly. The next Sunday afternoon, at the stated meeting of the session, I was presented with a resolution calling my sermon 'untimely and the references made to alleged sins of the congregation uncalled for.' In addition, the resolution, which was signed by seven of the nine elders and later repudiated by one of the signers, asked that I make 'no further political, social, or racial references from the pulpit, other than those that are required by the Bible,' and that I 'refrain from participating in any matter that might tend to involve the congregation in political, social, or racial controversy,' but should rather make 'the Gospel of Jesus Christ, and Him crucified, the sole topic of preaching at all times.'

"Although attendance at worship dropped drastically and never again reached the high level prior to the trouble, by the time I left the church sixteen months later, a reasonable harmony had been established. People still referred occasionally to 'that sermon' but without hostility."

Mr. Stanford is now minister of the Okolona Presbyterian Church in Louisville, Kentucky.[1]

TEXT: 1 JOHN 4:13-21

My dear friends and fellow Mississippians, this is a sermon that I really do not desire to preach and which I kept hoping would never have to be preached. But now I find that my hope was only wishful thinking, and my silence was only cowardice. And the result of that combination of cowardice and childishness has been tragic.

The horror at Ole Miss has been the result largely of Christian preachers who have not been preaching the whole counsel of God to the people of God. Those of us who have remained silent on a great and grave moral issue have lent support to those who have spoken out on the side of error and evil. We are now reaping what we have sown—the violence that comes from hatred: a hatred that we have allowed to develop because we never said that it is wrong.

But, at the same time, we never should have had to say that it is wrong. The Bible says it and says it quite strongly. The Bible knows no cowardice. It knows no childish wishes. It knows only what is true about God and about man and it speaks the truth.

This is what it says: "If any one says, 'I love God,' and hates his brother, he is a liar; for he who does not love his brother whom he has seen, cannot love God whom he has not seen."

This means simply: if you have hatred in your heart toward anyone, you do not have love in your heart for God.

During this past week we have seen the ugly head of hate reared in our state, and we have not liked what we have seen. Yet, we have not known that such a hideous monster has long been present here. We have not realized that he has been lurking beneath the surface for a great many years, rising now and again to give us a short, hurried view of his horror. But now at last he has burst through into full sight, and we have seen his hideous face. Few like what they have seen.

But there are some who like it, and there are many who have approved it, though not particularly liking it. And there are so many who have been saying, "This is what must happen if integration is tried here." So that is what did happen!

It is like any sin—if you think about it long enough and often enough, when it finally comes about you can enter into it joyfully and energetically because you have been doing it all along in your minds. But the deeper tragedy is that among those who have approved it, among those who have been preparing for it, among those who have done it, many are members of Christ's church. Some are members of the Presbyterian branch of Christ's church, and some are members of this particular church.

In other words, by giving ourselves into the hands of Christ, we have pledged ourselves to be servants of the Prince of Peace. But when the line has been firmly drawn, we find that we are not really the servants of the Prince of Peace at all. We find that we are more at home with the spirit of violence and war. To claim that such a spirit is a Christian spirit is to blaspheme the name of Christ.

All of us have done our share of hating during this past week. Some of us have hated Meredith for wanting to go to the university in the first place. Some of us have hated the Kennedys for attempting to force him into the school. And some of us have hated Barnett for disobeying the court order. But hatred has been in our hearts to one extent or another during this past week, and we have not tried to keep it from bursting forth.

Now we come today to the holy table of our Lord. We come to this spot where we thank God for his goodness to us, and where we are reminded of the sacrifice which Christ made of his own body and blood because of the hatred and violence of men.

And we are not just coming to this table by ourselves today. This is World-Wide Communion Sunday. We are approaching this table while people all around the world, people of varying hues of skin color and cultures and customs, are also approaching this table. We are coming to take the elements which mean to us that Christ has broken down the barriers which separate men from God and from one another. And we come knowing that we do not love all these people—knowing that some of them we hate.

The Bible says: "If any one says, 'I love God,' and hates his brother, he is a liar; for he who does not love his brother whom he has seen, cannot love God whom he has not seen."

If you come to this table today with unrepented sin upon your soul, you are doing your soul grievous damage. But if you repent of your sins and are sorry for them, then come joyfully to this table and learn of God's great love for you; then go forth and share that love with your neighbors.

Unto the Father, and unto the Son, and unto the Holy Spirit, be ascribed in the church all honor and glory, might, majesty, dominion, and blessing, now, henceforth, and for ever. Amen.

# The Testing of Our Faith

J. V. Cosby Summerell
First Presbyterian Church, Fayetteville, North Carolina
June 23, 1963

Located near the geographical border between "sandhill" and Piedmont North Carolina, the city of Fayetteville is a crossroad of tradition and change. The post-Revolutionary North Carolina General Assembly met four times in the town's State House, and here in 1789 it ratified the United States Constitution and chartered the University of North Carolina. Like few other cities in North Carolina, modern Fayetteville retains its feeling for the past, and its traditionalism is further accentuated by the fact that its markets are a major center of the tobacco and cotton economy of the region.[1]

Forces of change have also long been a part of the city's life. In 1877 the first state Negro teachers' college in the South was established here; and the modern descendant of this institution is part of the state university system. One of North Carolina's most progressive governors (1960-64) makes his home in Fayetteville, and the town was recently chosen as the site of a new Methodist college. But perhaps the strongest force for change in race relations has been the nearness of desegregated Fort Bragg, the largest military base (in area) in the United States. Becoming increasingly restless with merely living next door to desegregation, younger leaders in the Negro college and community by 1963 had organized a strong but mostly invisible protest movement. In June of 1963 for three intense weeks they led street demonstrations involving thousands of persons. The demonstrations were violent beyond many which took place in other parts of the state.

Fayetteville's mayor quickly formed a biracial committee to which Mr. Summerell was appointed. By midsummer the committee had taken steps toward the desegregation of a few eating places and other

77

public accommodations in the city. By the end of summer most observers believed that the tensions had been only superficially relaxed in
Fayetteville. "But since that time," says Mr. Summerell, "genuine
progress has been achieved in settling grievances. Housing for Negroes
has remained poor, but employment opportunities have markedly improved in the last two years."

The First Presbyterian Church, founded in 1800, is located downtown near the site of the ancient State House and on the edge of the
area where the demonstrations of 1963 took place. As one of fourteen
Presbyterian churches in a city of only 50,000, the First Church's history and present membership of 1500 give ample evidence of the
strength of Presbyterianism in this part of North Carolina.[2]

Mr. Summerell has been pastor of the church since 1961. For the
first two years of his ministry, he relates, his pulpit references to the
race question were occasional and indirect. But in June, 1963, "we
were beset by the demonstrations practically in front of our church
door. I debated within myself whether a sermon would help the situation or only make matters worse. One night I was caught inadvertently
in the strife on our main street. The tear gas, the angry mob, the im-
ported reinforcements for our local police, and the crackling tension
in the air suddenly made the whole crisis terribly real. The next day
this sermon was in the making. The initial reaction to the sermon by
members of the church was vocal, strong, and mixed. More than two
thousand copies were distributed to those requesting them. No dis-
senting members left the church, and no pressure of any consequence
was put upon me to reverse my position or to revert to pulpit silence
on this or any controversial issue. The church has an open-door policy,
and Negroes coming to worship will be admitted."

## TEXT: ACTS 21:26-39

This cannot be an ordinary hour of worship. This is no rou-
tinely ordinary day. It is a time of stress and strain, of tremendous
problems that touch every life and affect us all. What I say to you
today I must say. There are some among you who know that as
your minister a heavy burden has been upon my heart. If I tell
you that I am convinced that to evade the deep and depressing issues of these times would be an evasion of the holy vows I made
when I became an ordained minister of God, perhaps you will
understand. It is good to remember that when I was invited to be-

come your minister, I was assured of the freedom of this pulpit to preach the gospel as God leads me to understand it. I have tried not to abuse that responsibility and sacred trust. It is a mark of my confidence in you as a congregation concerned with seeking and finding the word and will of the Lord that I speak as I shall this morning.

This is very difficult for me because I know that what I shall try to say to you may be disturbing to many, and I would not want that. Some may be offended, and I do not want to offend anyone. Others quite conscientiously feel that I am abusing the privilege and responsibility of the pulpit. If this is true, I pray that God will make me aware of it, but with all my heart I have prayed about this, and I believe that this is his will. I am encouraged by the fact that so many of you have already expressed to me your compassionate understanding of the difficult place the ministry holds today. A number of you have come to talk with me about these things, and I am grateful. You have assured me of your prayers, and this means more than I can say. I want to discuss with you forthrightly—"The Testing of Our Faith."

I am a southerner by birth. I was born and educated in Virginia, and came to North Carolina a year and a half ago from a pastorate of six years in Alabama. There is in my heart a deep affection for the Negro race—an affection shared by true southern people. It bothers me quite a bit, as I know it bothers you, to know that these bonds of devotion between the white and Negro races are being tested and strained by the problems of today. Many of you have said warmly and sincerely, "Some of my best friends are Negroes." But obviously something is wrong. What is it? I would not presume to have the full answer to that. Wiser men than I are grappling with that—sociologists, anthropologists, statesmen, and politicians. But I can see clues to the answer. Unforgettable events have a way of stirring the complacent man to deeper thought and more purposeful action.

Several years ago I flew from Florence, Alabama, to Birmingham. Bad weather grounded the return flight, and I rode a late afternoon bus on the return journey. The bus stopped about 6:30 at a small crossroads community, and the driver announced that this was a fifteen-minute rest stop and that food was available here. A small hot dog stand was the only eating place in sight, and immediately it was crowded. I was one of the last to be served. I noticed that a young Negro couple were standing outside, and I watched them. Obviously, the young man was waiting until all others had been served. Then I saw him walk to the screen door, open it, and look at a waitress with a wordless question. I watched as she shook her head "no," and he shut the door and went back to his companion. It was time to eat and they could not eat. Impulsively, I bought two hamburgers and Coca-Colas and took them outside to the Negro couple. They thanked me profusely and he was anxious to pay, but I did not accept his money. Frankly, at that moment I was not proud of my race. When a white man came up to me and gruffly said, "What are you tryin' to do, mister, start trouble around here?", I was more confused, hurt, and ashamed than before. But I was glad that all of us on the bus, not just some of us, had had something to eat as we continued our journey.

The other incident happened more recently and here in Fayetteville, and was related to me by a leading businessman of our city. A leader of the disturbed Negro community sat in his office and talked about the place of the Negro in our society. He was making demands, and demands are rarely made or received graciously. The businessman was angry, but controlled his anger, and as he related the experience to me, he said, "That man had enough truth on his side to keep me from throwing him out." Interesting. What was the truth he was speaking of? The Negro said to the businessman something like this: "When World War II came, Americans white and black were drafted into the service of their country to defend it. We fought the Germans in Europe and the Japanese in the Pacific, and together we defeated them and the war was won. They were our enemies seeking to destroy us. Today a German or a Japanese can eat in any restaurant, sit anywhere he desires in any theatre, find employment in places where I, an American citizen and a Negro, cannot go. Is that fair?"

No, something is wrong. Our Negro friends grow weary of hearing the white man say, "I love the Negro. Some of my best friends are Negroes . . . but . . ."

Are you surprised when I say that this same wrongness, these same tensions, were felt deeply and painfully in the early church? We read this morning of a raging controversy centering around Paul's dealings with both Jews and Gentiles in the church.

Paul had arrived in Jerusalem at the time of Pentecost. The Jews had become suspicious of Paul, thinking that he had encouraged Jews to forsake their cherished customs and traditions. He had never done this, of course, but it is true that he had insisted that Gentile Christians need not observe ancient Jewish rites and ceremonies. To satisfy the Jews in this instance, Paul consented to sponsor four men who were taking their Nazirite vows. This was expensive and probably distasteful to Paul, but he did it in order to show his respect for Jewish law. For him it was merely a gesture. Since his conversion such distinctly Jewish acts had lost their relevance, but he did it because it meant much to Jews and did not violate his Christian convictions. Trouble arose, however, when the Jews, still not satisfied that Paul was with them and not against them, were persuaded by a mob of Asian Jews that Paul had taken Trophimus, a Gentile, into the sacred precincts of the Temple—a direct violation of Jewish law. The record says that the whole city was disturbed. Violence erupted. Paul was dragged outside the Temple, and the angry mob was about to kill him, when soldiers rushed in to restore peace and order. Does all this have a familiar sound to you? The commander of the troops asked who Paul was, and the crowd shouted back contradictory answers. How like a mob! Then, when Paul was being led to the safety of the barracks, a violent mob still following, shouting, "Kill him!", Paul asked the commander for permission to address the crowd. As a Christian, Paul used the time of crisis to preach the power and love of Christ.

He told them of his Jewish birth and of his higher education as a rabbi. Then of his miraculous conversion and of his becoming a new man in Christ, reborn, remade, the follower of a living religion with a living Lord. They listened in silence until he declared that God had led him to preach also to the Gentiles, and at this, the crowd became a mob again, shouting, "Away with such a fellow from the earth!"

There is much more about Paul's trial and ultimate deliverance. But the point is that Paul's conversion brought down the traditional barriers of race which he had been taught to recognize and respect. With Christianity, there came new and broader visions. It was from his experience as a man remade that Paul declared, "There is neither Jew nor Greek, there is neither slave nor free, there is neither male nor female; for you are all one in Christ Jesus" (Galatians 3:28).

So, you ask me what this means for us today, and I confess that I cannot tell you clearly and finally. We cannot superimpose Paul's situation on our own, obviously. And yet, there are guideposts here to help us find our way.

For one thing, *there is before us the inevitability of change.* How thankful we should be for that! Paul's travail was the growing pains of an expanding and maturing religious community. But change does not come easily. Human progress has come about by revolution that was painful, difficult, and dangerous. Thank God that there was a Paul to address the mob. My concern for the church in these times is that when the day of challenge and opportunity has come, the church by its silence and lack of Christian commitment will not lead. Many people have lost faith in the power of the Christian community to influence the world by its preaching and its witness toward peace and brotherhood. I have not lost that faith, and yet I am greatly concerned and deeply disturbed that apparently so many in the church feel that the problem of race is not a legitimate Christian concern, that the church should not "meddle." But Jesus said to us, "Ye are the light of the world" (Matthew 5:14, K.J.V.). The whole world is the concern of the Christian!

Secondly, I fear and am disturbed by *the modern tendency to see no disharmony between the oneness of Christ's gospel and the divisiveness of the world.* How can we do this, when the New Testament directs us to unity of faith and life? We cannot ignore the prayer of Jesus, "That they all may be one; as thou, Father, art in me, and I in thee, that they also may be one in us: that the world may believe . . ." (John 17:21, K.J.V.). We cannot evade the great commandment, "A new commandment I give unto you,

That ye love one another" (John 13:34, K.J.V.). Nor can we escape the stern and hard saying, "If you are offering your gift at the altar, and there remember that your brother has something against you, leave your gift there before the altar and go; first be reconciled to your brother, and then come and offer your gift" (Matthew 5:23-24). Most of all, we cannot disobey Christ's Great Commission, which makes the preaching of the gospel to the world our responsibility. How inconsistent that we should send missionaries to win black men in Africa and be so fearful that the black man will come into God's house here! Our Lord crossed traditional barriers of race and kind to minister to and to save a lost humanity. Can we, his church, hold the lines and refuse to overleap the barriers?

Thirdly, I am disturbed by *our unworthy attitudes toward others, and the suspicions we seem to cherish.* Suppose that the motive of a Negro going into a white church is not what it should be? How many of us could stand the test of honest and pure motive as we come into God's house? Do we not make jokes about those who come to church at Christmas and Easter to show off their fine clothing? Do we deny them entrance because their motives are not the best? Of course not. Rather, we take our cue from Christ who said, "I came not to call the righteous, but sinners to repentance" (Luke 5:32, K.J.V.). Let sinners come! Negro or white, the church is for the winning of souls and the remaking of men, all men. "My house shall be called a house of prayer for all peoples" (Isaiah 56:7; Mark 11:17).

Not as mere men, but as Christ's men must we face the tensions of our times. These times are for the testing of our faith. They are times for praying and for our *being* an answer to prayer. The Negro and the white together bear the guilt and share the blame for today's problems. Right is not on one side, nor is wrong. But this we have in common, we all need to stand in the presence of the Lord and Father of Jesus Christ and to confess: "All we like sheep have gone astray; we have turned every one to his own way; and the LORD has laid on him the iniquity of us all" (Isaiah 53:6).

# My Home Town

Lucius B. DuBose
First Presbyterian Church, Mullins, South Carolina
September 22, 1963

Mullins is an agricultural community of approximately 6,500 people. It has much in common with the county seat—Marion—and is the site of one of the largest tobacco markets in the United States.

The ratio of Negro to white population is roughly fifty-fifty. A few Negroes in the county own their own small farms; there is no Negro dentist or doctor; their dominant occupation is sharecropping. Though a few Negro leaders have been active in the South Carolina Human Relations Council, no public challenge to traditional patterns of segregation has been forthcoming in the county as a whole.

The First Presbyterian Church of Mullins, organized in 1901, has a membership of 270, composed largely of businessmen, farmers, professionals, and tobacco dealers. Mr. DuBose became pastor of the church in January, 1961. Two months after his arrival, at a joint meeting of elders and deacons, the officers of the church reaffirmed a previous policy not to seat Negro visitors at worship services; and the minister was asked to state his view on the question. Declaring his opposition to the policy, he conceded that for the present they would have to "agree to disagree."

A year later he made from the pulpit "a very timid probe into the area of the church's responsibility in the current social revolution, with no apparent repercussions." In the meantime, without publicity, he participated in the South Carolina Council on Human Relations and thus became well acquainted with several local Negro leaders.

The sermon below was preached in response to civil disorder ostensibly very remote from Marion County: the bombing of the Sixteenth Street Baptist Church in Birmingham, Alabama, on Sunday,

September 15, 1963, which resulted in the death of four girls and the injury of twenty other persons. The shock waves of this explosion reached Mullins, especially in the person of Mr. DuBose. "Because Birmingham was my home town," says he, "I felt that I could and must speak a personal word growing out of my own sense of involvement in this horrible tragedy."

Concerning the aftermath of the sermon, he writes: "Long before September 15, I had planned to be away from town for two weeks beginning September 22. This was unfortunate. While I was gone meetings were held, and when I returned a member of the session called on me to inform me that a joint meeting of the officers had decided that I should seek a call elsewhere as soon as practicable. No resolutions were recorded, no reason was given in writing. In the remaining two months of my time in Mullins I was to discover that the officers had succumbed to the pressure of a vocal minority. The majority, I discovered too late, remained loyal and heartbroken. Yet this majority over the years had allowed the church to be dominated by financially influential men whose cultural and economic anxiety made them the frightened defenders of the *status quo*. Such is the tragedy of many a congregation whose members do not ask soon enough what it is to be the Church of Jesus Christ."

After an interval of graduate seminary study, Mr. DuBose has become Associate Pastor of the Westminster Presbyterian Church in Nashville, Tennessee.

## TEXT: 1 CORINTHIANS 13

I am sure that you know the quickening of interest and feeling of pride that comes when the home town or home state achieves widespread or national renown. There is a sense of personal involvement in recognition afforded one who happens to come from the same place as you. Now you can say to the world, "That's where I was born, too." In a similar sense I have been personally very much involved of late in the news that has been making the headlines of press and television. I have had the recurring strange experience of seeing my personal past emerge out of television films, magazine and newspaper articles, as old familiar places and names and faces have made the news. For my home town, Birmingham, has suddenly burst into national and world prominence.

So, this morning I beg your indulgence to reminisce a bit about my home town. If what I have to say seems too personal, it is because I know no other way to express what has come home to me so deeply this week.

I remember a boy I met one summer at Camp Arrowhead, the Birmingham District Boy Scout Camp. We were together in a tent made up of boys, all strangers to each other, who had come to camp independent of any troop representation. Our bunks being next to each other, our ages being approximately the same, and perhaps because of a mutual loneliness, a relationship was formed between us that week which was as close to love as could be expressed by teen-age boys. Toward the end of the week I happened to ask him one day at rest period what church he attended and was surprised and, I must admit, a little regretful when he told me, "Temple Beth-el." I had not suspected that he was Jewish. I pushed it out of my mind, however, not seeing then what significance his religion could have for our friendship. On the last night of camp, as we filed down to the riverbank for the closing campfire, the realization that our time together was about over compelled us, in an innocent physical gesture, to hold hands. We were glad it was dark and no one could see us.

Summer ended and school began before I saw my friend again. I shall never forget the first time I encountered him in the school corridor. He was with a group of his Jewish friends and I was with my own crowd. I wanted to go to him and renew the friendship we had found that summer, but something stopped me. There seemed an impassable gulf between us, and we could only speak from a distance almost as strangers. And strangers we remained; though we passed in the halls every day, the friendship that we had found so meaningful was never renewed. Something warm and human in me died that day long ago when my courage failed me and I allowed a wall of community and personal prejudice to separate me from the one whom I had known and loved.

That happened at Ramsay High School. If you have been watching television lately, you have seen some pictures of Ramsay and its present-day students, turned ugly by the legacy of prejudice which I helped to pass on. Even back then when I was there, Ramsay was a sort of melting pot, its student body made up of Jews, Greeks, Italians, rough kids from the Five Points slums, and rich kids from the best element of society. It was probably because of this mixture that we had the best football team in the state. One of our heroes was a Greek boy who went on to make All-American in college. We thought he was great; we loved him . . . on the football field. But, of course, socially it was a different matter. It was all right going to school with Greeks, Italians, and Jews, especially if they could play football; but outside of school . . . well, they had their own churches and clubs and we had ours The problem at Ramsay now, you see, is not really new.

We didn't have any problem with Negroes back then. They had a good Negro high school in Birmingham. At least it looked pretty good from the outside. It was not nearly as nice as the five modern white high schools, but that was before 1954; and for a Negro school, Parker High was pretty good. The white community seemed to pride itself on having given the Negroes such a nice school. As I look back, however, and recall how my parents and their friends seemed almost compelled each time they passed it to talk about how nice it was, I wonder . . . Was it really pride, or was it to salve a guilty conscience?

One time I went with the choir of my church to visit a Negro Presbyterian church in the city. It was for a Sunday evening service; our minister preached and we sang the anthem. It was a good experience, and we went away feeling that we had participated in a real act of Christian brotherhood. I don't recall being particularly bothered by the fact that the visit could never be repaid.

The church was a big part of my life back then. I loved my church, "The Old First Church" of Birmingham, the oldest church in the city, built when Birmingham was only a village. My family and I drove many miles downtown every Sunday morning to worship, passing on the way some of the worst slums in the city. But I never saw much connection between my dutifully performed weekly worship and my concern, or absence of concern, for the destitute of my city. Nor did it occur to me that our church had any responsibility toward the people who lived in the low-income housing project only two blocks from our church door. After all, they were not our kind of people; they would not have felt at home in the "Old First Church." But I wonder . . . why wouldn't they?

I am not condemning my church or my home town. I owe everything I am to my church and to the great Christian heritage it passed on to me. For all its blind spots, "Old First Church" was, and is, a great church. I shall forever be indebted to Birmingham for the excellence of its schools. All my good memories of youth focus in that smoky, young, immature, sprawling industrial city, stretching out in the valley between two mountain ranges. It is an irreplaceable part of my past and an inevitable part of my present. That is why this past week I have felt so deeply the tragedy of Birmingham.

For Birmingham—"The Magic City," they call it, because of the unparalleled rapid growth of its iron and steel industry—has become a leading manufacturer of something besides steel. It has become a leader in the production of homemade bombs. Last Sunday that new industry came of age. The people of Birmingham—my people, my friends, my relatives—brought together such raw materials as they have produced over the years, the accumulated blindness and prejudice of decades, and out of it constructed a crude but efficient bomb, and together they planted it in the basement of the Sixteenth Street Baptist Church and with it murdered four little girls who were studying their Sunday school lesson.

The pride of a great city died when that bomb went off. Birmingham, a name already besmirched but not perhaps beyond cleansing, became in that frightful moment last Sunday an ugly word. It will be many years before my home town recovers its self-respect, before people like me can say again with pride, "Birmingham is my home."

But I wonder, must my city alone bear the stigma of this awful deed? Surely no one doubts that it is the people of Birmingham who are guilty of this hideous act, and not merely the fear-crazed madmen who actually planted the dynamite. The blame rests upon the mayor and city council who vacillated too long between the right and the expedient; upon newspaper editors who did not stir hard enough at the thickened conscience of their city; upon every minister of the gospel who failed to translate that gospel into acts of love; upon every parent who buttoned up his children's minds with prejudice and taught them to hate what they never understood; upon the decent people of Birmingham who publicly abhorred the violence of the Ku Kluxers and "nigger baiters" but secretly hoped that they would win; upon every citizen, black or white, who poured hatred instead of love upon the seething cauldron of a troubled city. Surely these *are* the guilty; but are they to be isolated in their guilt from the rest of us? What of the rest of the people of Alabama? Does not the whole state share the burden of its chief city? And what of the rest of the South? Birmingham is above all else a southern city, born out of the Civil War, its first steel foundries built to make cannon for the Confederacy. The public attitudes which spawned last Sunday's savage act are not peculiar to Birmingham; they belong to Mississippi and Georgia and South Carolina and the other southern states, as well. Then, surely Birmingham is not to be singled out as the sole resting place of blame.

Besides being called "The Old First Church," my home church is also known as "The Church of the Bells," because in its steeple is a magnificent Belgian carillon which, when it was installed many years ago, was one of the finest in the country. Every Sunday morning for as long as I can remember, the church organist has gone to the church tower and there, at the huge manual console of the carillon, has played on the bells a concert of hymns for the resting city. I read in the newspaper that every day at noon during this week the church bells of Birmingham have tolled in mourning and repentance. How sad! To think of that beautiful carillon, created to run and trill the scale in exciting and joyous harmonies, now reduced to tolling in sonorous funeral cadence the shame of a city!

There are a lot of churches in Birmingham; that must have been quite an impressive sound each noon this week—and yet, a sort of pathetic sound, a hollow sound, an empty sound. For after all, however well intentioned, the ringing of church bells is a rather pitiful gesture *after* something like this has happened. It makes one wonder what those bells have been ringing about all these years. It makes one wonder what the churches of Birmingham, and the churches of the whole South, have been talking about all these years. It makes one wonder if it's too late for them to recover their lost opportunity to *do* something meaningful and constructive about human relations, to break the Christian gospel out of the spiritual vacuum in which it has too long reverberated and to allow it to transform our attitudes and actions. Will the churches of Birmingham, the churches of the South, *this* church, ever begin to take seriously the implications of Jesus' teaching about love for neighbor? Will we ever understand what he was saying in the simple story of the Samaritan? Will our church bells ever ring out over our towns in genuine invitation? Or must they wait until such a time as this to toll our failure—to send out sad signals of our shame and guilt?

# Christian Response to Racial Revolution

James McBride Dabbs
Cherokee Presbytery, meeting at
Acworth Presbyterian Church, Acworth, Georgia
April 21, 1964

The following address breaks the pattern of this volume in three significant respects: it was delivered by a ruling elder rather than a teaching elder of the southern Presbyterian Church; it was not originally considered a "sermon"; and it was spoken not to a single local congregation but to a presbytery.

The pattern is appropriately broken at this point, for as many significant reasons: Presbyterianism as a system of church government is founded on the idea of the parity of the eldership. Moreover, though the parity chiefly concerns equality of voting strength in upper church courts, the ordination vows of both kinds of elders are so nearly alike as to suggest that ruling elders with the gifts are permitted to be theologians. Finally, Presbyterianism is "connectional" in its idea of church government, and this connectionalism is embodied very strongly in the presbytery. Despite some contrary indications in this volume, Presbyterians officially reject the theory of congregational autonomy, especially as regards the calling and the dismissing of a minister.

An additional reason for including James McBride Dabbs in this collection is that, for the past fifteen years of his writing and lecturing, he has been a unique theologian-at-large, interpreting the South to itself and to the world. Living on a plantation replete with Spanish moss and pillared ante-bellum house near Mayesville, South Carolina, Dr. Dabbs first became involved actively in the race question through his "shock at the bad manners of the South Carolina legislature, which, in

91

1945, tried to make the Democratic Primary a gentleman's club excluding Negroes." His mating of a plea for "manners" with a plea for Negro voting rights, in a letter to the Columbia newspaper, was to prove typical of his skill at pitting the best in southern culture against the worst. Since 1945 his execution of this maneuver has taken him into the Presidency of the South Carolina Council of Human Relations (1948-53), the Presidency of the Southern Regional Council (1957-63), membership in the Committee of Southern Churchmen, appointment to the Presbyterian U.S. General Assembly's Permanent Committee on Christian Relations, and authorship of three books and many articles interpretive of the South. His book *The Southern Heritage* won the 1958 Brotherhood Award of the Southern Conference of Christians and Jews. He holds the honorary degree of Doctor of Humane Letters from Morehouse College.

The following address was spoken to a presbytery whose boundaries take in the northwest corner of Georgia. The area would therefore be considered by most Georgians as having a somewhat less critical race problem than do counties south of Atlanta. The address is included here as the timely word of a lay theologian who, in the post-Oxford, post-Birmingham year of 1964, was able to offer ruling and teaching elders a positive Christian interpretation of civil disorder. Such interpretation has been classically rare among southerners.

TEXT: JOHN 5:17

Alfred North Whitehead has remarked that two lines of one of our great hymns sum up man's perennial response to the world:

"Change and decay in all around I see;
O Thou who changest not, abide with me."[1]

I would call your attention especially to that first line: "Change and decay in all around I see." We tend to equate change with decay. We are poor creatures, frightened by the vastness of the world, holding on to the scenes and the faces we have known, wrapping the roots of our being about particular things and people. It is man's way "to hold on with the heart." But as Christians we also recognize that God is somehow in the world now, in these changing places and faces, that he is the God of the living, an ever-present God, that as Jesus said, "My Father is working still, and I am working" (John 5:17). The creation of the world still goes on.

It is the duty of the Christian then to ask, What is God doing in the world now? And particularly, What is God doing in the revolutions of our time? Looked at superficially, the world is going to pieces, around the globe, even here in the South. Looked at more deeply, it may be merely shaking itself; that is, God may be shaking the foundation, to make clear to us which structures are built upon sand and which upon the rock. And though such periods are always periods of disorder, new structures arise, through which men create and find order. The old structures give way, not because men are essentially chaotic; we do have chaos in us, but we are essentially social creatures, creatures of orderly institutions, and the old structures give way because, for all their apparent orderliness, they rest upon spiritual disorder.

Consider our racial situation in the South. In recent years we have seen or we have heard much of Negroes sitting at lunch counters reserved for whites, requesting service. Though these people, usually young, sat there quietly, many of us said their actions were disorderly. We meant that they were not in accordance with the accepted order and custom of the South. The Negro was getting out of his place, and in the South this by definition is disorder. But who made the order—of segregation, of the Negro kept permanently on the bottom rung of the ladder? Did the world-rejuvenating spirit of democratic America make it? I know there are those who argue that God was the first segregationist. I am not going to try to refute them. You can prove anything from the Bible, if you take only chapter and verse. The devil, too, can quote Scripture. That's one reason I hesitate to quote it. I can only say of those who argue like this, I pity them; nor do I understand how their spirit is any reflection of the compassionate spirit of Jesus and the redemptive love of God. So far as I am concerned, segregation denies the basic historic thrust of American democracy. Therefore I oppose it as an American who believes in democracy. It also denies the compassionate, universal spirit of Christianity. Therefore I oppose it as a Christian.

But let us come back to those young people sitting quietly at the lunch counter. These young people, though quiet, are committing an officially disorderly act. It's always dangerous to guess what may be in people's hearts and minds; but my guess is that, beneath the excitement, the fear, the tense nerves, there has been in these demonstrators a sense of order and quiet which previously they had seldom known. They had never agreed to be segregated, to be shunted out of the mainstream of our culture. Nobody asked them. We white people had the power, and we used it. We said that we were using it to preserve the peace, but they knew we were using it because we thought we were better than they. Put yourself in the Negro's place, and imagine the disorder this stirs up in your mind. When, therefore, these young people rose against the social order, they were expressing an inner sense of order that had been denied and trampled upon for a long time.

Segregation is going now for many reasons, but most of all because it rested upon spiritual disorder. The physical and social world in which our fathers lived was so confused and threatening, so close to chaos, that they were induced to hammer out some kind of order regardless of what it did to their spirits. We today have no such excuse. So far as the local problems of the South are concerned, we live in far happier times. (I do not forget the atomic cloud.) Being therefore less constrained by circumstances to enforce an iron order, we are better able to sense the inner disorder that this outer order causes. If now, simply out of complacency or out of selfish desire to maintain our privileged position, we refuse to consider and weigh the inner disorder, we shall surely be condemned. In the past, God may have winked at our racial misdeeds; but now he is looking at us. We continue the disorder at our peril.

The racial revolution, which is showing its influence even in the South, is world-wide. We ought to remember this when we are prone to blame a few individuals for the radical changes which are taking place. I do not say that because it is world-wide it is necessarily God's direct will. But if we believe in God's providence, I think we could hardly believe that such a world-wide movement was taking place in opposition to providence.

The world racial revolution is primarily a revolt of so-called "natives" against imperial control. They are now demanding freedom, respect, and a fairer share in the goods they have helped to produce. As Christians how can we deny them this? Indeed, we should be pleased, both as democratic Americans and as Christians, that these millions are coming of age, and are asking to be treated like men.

The Negroes of the South, and of America, are strictly a part of this revolution. In a certain sense the Negroes of America are colonials. When the structure of colonialism collapses throughout the world it is at least appropriate, if not inevitable, that it should collapse here.

In spite of the resistence with which many southerners and indeed many Americans greet this inevitable collapse, the will to defend segregation steadily grows weaker. Why? Because year by year we move further from its bitter causes in Reconstruction. We have less reason to support it. Also, because we, too, are moved by a zeal for democracy, and cannot support from the heart this undemocratic practice. Finally, because the will with which men support any institution is directly related to their hope of maintaining it. Daily the hope of maintaining segregation grows less.

I do not need to emphasize the fact that this racial revolution is occurring throughout the United States. It may have begun in the South; its chief locus may still be the South; it is certainly evident now in the big cities across the nation; but there are good grounds for believing that the South will resolve this problem before the rest of the nation does. The reason, simply, is that southerners, white and colored, have all lived with it, and with one another, and in the process have learned far more of the answers than at the moment they realize.

There are the answers evident, for example, in the non-violent nature of the Negro's revolution. It is true that the Negroes may have adopted the strategy of non-violence partly because historically the South has been prone to violence and quick on the trigger. Non-violence seemed the most practicable method of challenging the system. But they have adopted it also because they have learned a patience which is rooted in the Christian religion, and they have a Christian—and a southern—faith in their white neighbors. This non-violent revolution is occurring not solely because we have been both undemocratic and unchristian in our treatment of Negroes, but also because we have been, however limitedly, Christian. Many southerners have talked as if the southern way of life was simply segregation, discrimination, and the Negro "in his place" at the bottom. This is to sell the South sadly short; this is to make ourselves out far worse than we are.

As selfish, as complacent, as proud as we have been, there has also been God's grace working among us. It is the presence of grace that gives to this revolution its peculiar character. As Christians we should ponder this. Is not grace the key word in Calvinistic theology? And yet today we look around us and are disturbed, irritated, angry, frightened. Let us trust God and look closer. We shall find in the Negro movement qualities and attitudes which neither the Negroes nor the whites intended, but which have simply grown out of the life of the South. If these unplanned attitudes are commendable, I should say they illustrate the grace of God.

Let us consider again those young people sitting at lunch counters in the first faint dawn of their movement. Everybody has noticed their excellent manners, often in such contrast to the unmannerliness of the white delinquents who stood around. Is not good manners the quality on which the South, justly or unjustly, has prided itself most? Were not these Negro youngsters, then, by this standard, good southerners?

But ah, you say, they were violating racial etiquette. Well, they were. In the democratic world into which they had been born, stirred by the wind of freedom which at long last had blown to them across the pages of the Bible, they saw no place now for racial etiquette. They did not declaim against it; they simply discarded it. For they were engaged, however quietly, in a revolution. And perhaps the essence of this revolution is a redefinition of the great words of the South. We have been a people of great words: courtesy, honor, integrity, truth, courage, love. We are being asked now to look at these words and see what they mean for today. Maybe now, in this revolution, the South will not be lost but found. Found for its place in the modern world.

These Negro youngsters came with good manners and also with a religious heart. As I read the history of the South, we are generally a people of deep religious convictions and of good manners. But time and again I sense a flaw, a gap, between the manners and the religion. There is always some gap between culture and any world religion, Christianity most of all. In the South, however, the gap was too great. There was a complex social culture, a rich web of manners, covering the surface of life, shutting off from daily view the mystery, the violence, the terror of life. It was hoped that individualistic Protestant religion would take care of this, but a highly social life and a highly individualistic religion hardly go together.

Look again: here, in these well-mannered, quiet-spirited, committed youngsters the gap is closed. They are at home in this world and in another. They are at home in this world because they are at home in another. Just as they adopted southern manners but discarded racial etiquette, so they combined with the deep piety, the personal religion of the South, a sense of social justice drawn straight from the great prophets but never stressed in the South before. They are not revolutionary in being religious; the South is religious. They are revolutionary in combining with the religious piety of the South a religious demand for social justice which the South could never make.

Why could it not make it? Because of slavery, and, afterwards, of segregation. We may have been hypocrites—all men are, more or less; but we weren't such hypocrites as to preach social justice while maintaining slavery and segregation. What did we do then? We stressed love, with all its variations: kindliness, courtesy, good humor. Though I think love is the root and the fruit of the universe, in this world love needs justice to support it. Try to express it without at the same time striving for justice, and you get sentimentality. Southerners are admittedly sentimental. We like the songs at twilight, the Carolina moons, the sunset all misty through the Spanish moss; but we ought to know when we are sentimental, saving the mood perhaps for those moments when day fades into night, not trying to use it at high noon. We southerners try it at high noon, and in regard to our perennially most

urgent problem, race. We see the Negro through a haze; we had
to see the Negro like this; we couldn't bear to see him as he was.

And now he comes, in the best manners of the South, *re-
defined,* with the religiously committed heart of the South, *rede-
fined,* trying to unite courtesy and Christianity, piety and justice.

Is not this God's most gracious Spirit giving us at last what we
tried so long unsuccessfully to get? But giving it to us in a form
nobody had planned or even dreamed of? The Negro was brought
here to speed the production of tobacco and cotton. In our last
desperate defense of slavery we said—our own Dr. Thornwell
said it[2]—that God had brought the Negro here in order that he
might receive the message of salvation. Maybe Dr. Thornwell
was right. Maybe the Negro has received through us, by God's
grace, a clearer realization than we ourselves had. This may be
another case of the stone the builders rejected. If it is, it is a sharp
rebuke to our pride. For we shall have gained what we always
strove for, but by a means we neither desired nor planned, so that
we find it hard now to accept. It is hard, brethren, to accept the
grace of God.

As I see the racial revolution in the South, then, it is the Spirit
of God working for freedom against bondage, and it is the spirit
of the South discarding old evils, creating new goods. We should
welcome the revolution, both as Christians and as southerners—
as southern Christians. If we cannot welcome it completely, we
should at least not fear it. "All things work together for good to
them that love God."[3] Though our world is changing it is not
necessarily decaying. "My Father is working," said Jesus, "and I
am working." Let us work with him.

# The March on Washington

Carl R. Pritchett
Bethesda Presbyterian Church, Bethesda, Maryland
September 1, 1963

History attests that Presbyterians, southern and northern, were among the most unanimous and militant supporters of the American Revolution.[1] But history will not record that Presbyterians were such supporters of the "Second American Revolution": the integration of the Negro into American life. This fact is reflected in the following two sermons, which portray southern Presbyterian ministers' own personal struggle with the problem of bridging the gulf between certain elements of their inherited Presbyterianism and their new sense of God's judgment in the Civil Rights Movement.

Bethesda, Maryland, is a suburb of Washington, D.C. Most of its residents are employed in U.S. government agencies. The Presbyterian church which named the community was founded in 1820 and now numbers a membership of some 1200. Like the city of Washington itself, Bethesda is a meeting point of north and south. A southern Presbyterian church, therefore, does not blend simply with the surrounding culture. As Dr. Pritchett testifies, an occasional visitor, learning that the church is "southern" in affiliation, immediately dismisses the idea of becoming a member under the impression that it is segregationist. "Some of our southern brethren," says he, "would find it hard to believe that the mere fact that we are southern could be a handicap!"

Though few Negro families live in Bethesda (a fact significant for future chapters of the Civil Rights story), this church has been open to all people for many years, and occasionally Negro families are in the worshiping congregation.

A native of North Carolina, Carl Pritchett's pilgrimage in race relations, up to a point, resembles that of many other southern Presby-

terian ministers of this century: "Born with a good case of race prejudice," he lost it intellectually at college and seminary. As pastor of the
Davidson College Presbyterian Church (Davidson, N.C.), he repeatedly preached the New Testament view of race relations to several
generations of college students. Then, a significant step beyond a pulpit ministry on the matter was taken by him one Sunday in 1950 when,
at the sound of fire engines, he dismissed the church service early and
followed the siren a hundred yards away to a burning shack in Brady's
Alley. As he took in the full meaning of that burning shack, he says,
"I decided to go to the end of the road on the issue. We cleaned up the
alley, and we improved the water and sewage situation of the whole
town. We built thirteen homes that are still attractive, and we worked
out a local finance scheme so that these people could own a home.
None of them was given a nickel. It was the only time I have ever had
to take a sleeping pill"—one price of getting the church involved in the
real estate business.

The price of getting it involved in the March on Washington is the
subject of the following sermon, preached to the Bethesda church the
Sunday following the March. That the step from Brady's Alley to the
Washington Mall should be a long one for any man will appear
strange only to those readers who do not share with Dr. Pritchett a
Protestant and/or southern upbringing with its fear of "mass demonstrations." "Now that it is past," he remembers, "it is difficult to re-
construct the atmosphere of real fear here in Washington. People predicted riots and bloodshed. People in Bethesda were right here glued
to their television sets. As everyone knows now, the actual event was
a revelation of magnificent spirit and discipline. Everything I believe
most strongly about God, the church, and my country was symbolized
there in an amazing way." A few members of the Bethesda church
were themselves in the March. After the sermon most of the members
supported the minister's right to participate; a few registered protest
by reducing contributions. Published before in a Presbyterian periodi-
cal,[2] the sermon resonates with the inner struggle of countless other
Protestant ministers in the nineteen-sixties.

TEXT: ROMANS 12

A few months ago, Dr. John Rock, a medical doctor and a
Roman Catholic, published a book entitled *The Time Has Come*.
It deals with the thorny problem of birth control, as seen by the
Roman Catholic Church and by the medical profession. In the in-

troduction to the book he tells about a conversation between himself when he was fourteen years old and a certain Father Finnick. As they rode together down a country road near Marlborough, Massachusetts, the quiet and saintly priest turned to him and said, "John, always stick to your conscience. Never let anyone else keep it for you." He drove a little further and said, "And I mean anyone else." All of his life he has remembered what Father Finnick said to him. That's why he wrote his book. It was a matter of conscience.

That was exactly my trouble with the March on Washington. I could not turn my conscience over to anyone else. I could not let the Civil Rights leaders, the Council of Churches, the Presbyterian Church, or this congregation keep my conscience. I sometimes do not know what to do with my conscience. It is so difficult to know what is right and wrong. Things are not black and white to me any more. I live in the gray—always in the gray. There are times when I make my way out of the gray into the white. At still other times I find myself in the black. Whether I stand in the white or the black I am not always absolutely sure I am right. Wherever I stand I have discovered that I must stand as a penitent. Not only so, but I like to be able to do something more than to take a stand. I like to know just why I am there and not somewhere else. That is why I almost missed the March on Washington.

Dr. Eugene Carson Blake said, "We come late, late we come." I was so late I almost didn't get there. I did not decide to take part in the March until the morning before the March for Jobs and Freedom. This seemed a little strange to me, because my heart was with the cause. For thirty years I have identified myself with the cause of justice for the Negro both in society and in the church. My heart was with them, but I had trouble with my head and my feet. I had difficulty in sifting the facts and issues until I had enough clarity of understanding for a judgment. I just couldn't seem to get my feet out in a public street. I am not used to settling a problem in the street. A few nights before, I had said to a friend over the phone, "You do what you think is right and I will do what I think is right. Everyone's duty is not the same. If I were to

shuffle down the street to prove to myself or to someone else that
I believe in freedom and jobs for the Negro people I would be a
hypocrite. I have stood for these things for thirty years. I just
can't do it." But I did. I want to tell you why I had so much difficulty and how I finally made it to the street.

I had received a telegram from three ministers in our Presbytery whom I respected. It was not a pressure device by subtle
ecclesiastics. I had been under that kind of pressure and had rebelled against it. I just can't stand that kind of awkward attempt
to force my conscience and judgment. But, this telegram inviting
me to come to the Church of the Pilgrims and worship God I
knew to be sincere. It put the possibility in a different perspective.
I made a phone call to get a little more information and shortly
thereafter I decided to get out in the street. I doubt that I would
have made it to the street if I had not gone first into the church.

So, we met at the Church of the Pilgrims the morning of the
March. Our worship was conducted by three of our ministers, all
properly gowned. We did everything but take up the collection.
The pastor of the church had charge of the service. He is a southerner. I have known his family for years. He is as orthodox as
anyone I know. He never has been a member of the Communist
party. He has never been in a riot. He explained to us why we
were there in restrained theological and biblical language. He
did leave out one thing. He forgot the lecture against violence,
but that's about all he left out. He said everything else that had to
be said to us. Another Presbyterian led us in a prayer of confession. It was thoughtful, probing, and painful. I sat there with my
head bowed and said, "Yes, Lord, that is exactly the way it is with
us."

We really didn't know how to march very well. We had no
practice. We didn't keep step. Someone had printed on a white
cardboard, nailed to a slender piece of wood, "Presbyterian,
U.S." This was the sign we marched behind. As we walked down
the street we were talking with one another. The streets were like
Sunday morning, quiet and empty. I said to my companion, "You
know, I have a feeling it's going to be like church." An alert
young Negro student came by with some flags which he sold for a

dollar to help the expenses of the March. I bought one and carried it throughout the parade. I had vowed I would not wave a silly banner, but there I was with one to wave. There wasn't anyone to wave to except the television crews or the policemen. There were no spectators. You were either in the parade or you weren't there. There was no one to riot with. We were demonstrating before the conscience of America, which is invisible.

By the time we got to Constitution Avenue it was full of people moving toward the Lincoln Memorial. It was pretty hot out there in the sun. Some people took off their shoes and put their feet in the pool. After we got settled some began to eat their prepared lunches. I hadn't even thought about lunch. I was too busy trying to make up my mind about going on the March. A fellow minister opened up his briefcase and offered me a sandwich. You never know what is in a briefcase in Washington!

After all of the predictions of violence, it was quite startling to observe the temper of the crowd. I never felt crowded or pushed. I could have carried a baby in my arms with perfect safety. I did not see a single person angry or irritable or impolite. I read later that a Negro woman told a reporter, "They treat you different here. A white man stepped on my foot and said, 'Excuse me,' and I said, 'Certainly.' I believe that is the first time a white person has ever been kind to me." That was the mood of what some people called a "mob." It was an unforgettable experience. Often as I sat there and listened to the moving speeches and enjoyed the hootenanny atmosphere, I shook my head and said to myself in wondering disbelief, "And I almost missed it!"

Why was it so hard for me to get into the March? It certainly was not that I was afraid to stand up and be counted on the race issue. I have done that for thirty years in every pulpit I have occupied. Every congregation I ever served has heard more about the race issue than they wanted to hear. I have been called a "nigger lover" by the wife of a white man who had tried to rape the daughter of a Negro Presbyterian elder. The girl's father was a friend of mine and I had gone to that Carolina Court House as a character witness. When the wife spat out the words my bones turned to water. I consider the words a high compliment, but as a southerner I knew the meaning of that epithet. I have engaged in a housing project for Negro people, I have attended Race Relations Institutes and steeped myself in the literature on every aspect of the problem. I have followed the developments of our present situation with close attention. In spite of all of this, I barely managed to get in the March.

I had so much trouble getting into the March because my participation meant more than walking down the street with a flag in my hand. It symbolized my intellectual, moral, and emotional acceptance of the new racial situation. This was not easy for me. Demonstrations in the streets, pickets at a business establishment, sit-ins in a restaurant, are just not my way of settling problems. I do not like to get out in the street with a problem. My way is to read a book, ponder its meaning, and pace the study. My way is to engage in a discussion in a committee, take a vote, and abide by the majority decision. My way is to be regulated in an assembly by parliamentary procedure and governed by the official position of the group. My way is submission of disputes to arbitration, negotiation, and the courts of law. My way is to stand in the pulpit and appeal to reason, conscience, and the heart. It is just not my way to get out in the street with a problem of justice and freedom and economics. I still do not think it is the best way or a good way. It just happens to be the place where the problem is at present. If we live with the problem we must in imagination, spirit, sympathy, and perhaps even bodily get out in the streets.

I finally said to myself, "So far as I was able, I tried to settle it in the pulpit. I tried to settle it in the church assemblies and by negotiation, but it could not be done. The church could have settled this the way it ought to be settled, but it did not do it. The church could have abolished slavery and did not. The church in Reconstruction days could have moved gradually to grant freedom of opportunity and dignity to the Negro and did not do it." When the 1954 Supreme Court decision was made I said, "This is the time. Now we have a great opportunity to live up to our American creed. This is a great hour for the church." In the town in which I lived we organized a Christian Human Relations Council to help us to understand and contribute to the desegregation of

American life. I talked with the mayor of the town. I went to see the editor of the papers. But it was not long before the politicians made up their minds. The climate changed. Many in the church did not want us even to meet on the premises to discover our Christian duty. We had a pitiful meeting or two in the basement of a municipal building and tried to close it up with some semblance of human dignity. I left town because I had become a problem to the church. I came to this church because I thought I could be a free man in this pulpit and save my soul. I do not wish to disrupt the unity of the church, but if I cannot preach what I think is the word of God I will not preach.

So, the church cannot complain that the problem is now in the streets. The church forced it out in the streets. It will not do for us to point out to all what is dangerous and wrong with this present attempt at a solution in the streets. We forced it into the streets and it will not come back to the negotiating table until the demonstrations in the streets have given the Negro Civil Rights leaders enough influence at the table.

If I should ever feel that my place is physically out in the street, it will be because my church has forced me out of the sanctuary, the church courts, and into the street. If it embarrasses the church that one of its ministers is in jail it is just too bad. All of these possibilities are now with me an open question.

I don't want you to get nervous and think I have completely lost my balance. I have no present plans to demonstrate. I don't think I would make a good picket. By the time I had finished with my thorough investigation the demonstration would probably be over. I think I could picket a mean-spirited atheist who sells liquor to teen-agers. But, if I discovered that his poor wife was dying with cancer and his teen-age daughter was humiliated, I would probably take some aspirin and make a pastoral call.

One reason I have been so offended by recent events is that the moderate among the Negro people seems to have disappeared. The restraint and public criticism of some unwise and irresponsible demonstrations have not been evident. I have wondered if the Civil Rights leaders have lost the capacity to be self-critical. If they had reservations and scruples they seem to have settled them in some way and almost forgotten the white moderate. They want us there beside them, but we will march behind their leadership if we march with them. This will take some doing. We do not know them so well. So much misinformation and suspicion has been scattered about that we will have a confusing time trying to sift truth from falsehood. We may not like this, but what we like will not change the hard fact. This is one of the jolting, shocking facts in the new situation.

Another major reason I had so much difficulty in getting into the March on Washington was my fear of violence. Now, I am fascinated by violence. I am perfectly capable of violence myself. But I am afraid of it. I have suffered with people who have committed crime in a moment of passion and violence. I have seen their futile tears of remorse. I know that when violence comes in the streets reason is clouded, conscience is driven from the throne, injury and death can result. In all of the tumult and confusion of some demonstrations it is hard to distinguish between the violence which is caused by the innocent and by the guilty. The threat of violence can never be a justification for the deprivation of constitutional rights. This would be utterly wrong and mischievous. But we love law and order.

One of the leaders of the March made what I thought was a very perceptive remark. He said, "The reason the Negro today believes in direct non-violence is that the American people are more committed to law and order than to justice." I think this is correct, especially if it is justice for someone else. But there is a deeper reason we stand for law and order. It is through our law and order that the common idea of justice is expressed. Ordinarily law and order are essential to justice. The problem of the Negro is that law and order are against his constitutional rights. He feels that he has a right and higher duty to rebel against the law that is in itself unjust. He feels often like the Apostles who said, "We must obey God rather than men" (Acts 5:29). That decision should be reserved for the most clear and ultimate issues. The Negro people think this is such an issue.

Perhaps there are people present today who are saying to

themselves, "Just what can I do to help solve the racial crisis?" Let me make a few simple suggestions:

1. You can pray that God will help you overcome your racial prejudice. I have been praying against my racial prejudice for thirty years and I am not through. If I claimed to be without race prejudice it would be like claiming to be without sin. So, you can desegregate yourself through prayer.

2. You can pray for the Civil Rights leaders. They have a growing power and need your prayers. If you think they are often wrong, pray that God will help them to find the truth and do what is right. Fortunately, they are Christian men, so far as I know. Some of them are Christian ministers.

3. You can speak up and speak out when it is courteous and appropriate to do so. Your opinion counts. You can write your congressman.

4. You can judge the Civil Rights leaders and the Civil Rights movement in the same way you judge the Christian church— with discrimination. We need to substitute rational discrimination for racial discrimination. I have found the best people I know in the church and the worst. I have found the most psychologically mature and the queerest personalities in the church. I admire Peter, John, and Paul and am saddened by Judas Iscariot. I will not desert Christ or get out of the church because it is not exactly like I want it to be. Now that this is clear to me I have no special difficulty in adjusting myself to the necessity for individual, responsible judgments concerning anything in these tumultuous events.

Perhaps there are also people present today who do not conscientiously believe in either a nonsegregated church or a nonsegregated society. I understand this point of view and the feelings of people who have it. I was born in it and have relatives who hold to it strongly. I do not wish to impose my views on you any more than I want you to impose your views on me. I have often thought of a remark of William Penn, the Quaker founder of Pennsylvania. He was a pacifist. He had taken off his sword. One day he was talking with a man who would not take off his sword because he did not believe in pacifism. Penn smiled and said, "Friend, wear it as long as thou canst." So, I say to you, "Keep this view as long as you can. Keep it until you can honestly change your mind and maintain your integrity. Keep it even until the day you die. But the day you die the time of your choice will be over. When you get to heaven, as I am sure you will, you will find nothing else but a nonsegregated church in a nonsegregated society. Why not, then, add this to all the other joys of heaven—that it will be exactly the way you want it to be?"

# *I Have a Dream*

James I. Lowry, Jr.
Meadowview Presbyterian Church, Louisville, Kentucky
September 8, 1963

If southern white Presbyterians find difficulty identifying themselves with the Civil Rights Movement, one important reason is their lack of personal relationships with Negro churchmen. Of over 900,000 communicants in the denomination, only 6,339 are Negroes; of some 4,000 southern Presbyterian ministers, only 44 are Negroes; and of some 4,000 congregations, only 74 are predominantly Negro in membership. No one knows how many at least tokenly integrated congregations are in the denomination; but by the end of 1964 only 38 of the 74 Negro congregations were desegregated even on the presbytery level. Leaders of the remaining 36 congregations (located chiefly in five Deep South states) made organizational contact with the denomination chiefly at the level of the annual General Assembly.[1] Thus on almost all levels of denominational life, but most especially in the local community, the argument for a white congregation's involvement in the Civil Rights struggle is stated, if at all, by persons who do not have that argument "in their bones," because they are white rather than Negro persons. One may conclude, therefore, that a personal and social vacuum has hindered southern Presbyterians (and many other Protestants) from coming to grips with the Civil Rights Movement in theological and churchly terms.

The origins of the following sermon point to the reality of this vacuum. The Meadowview Presbyterian Church is one of 24 southern Presbyterian congregations in Louisville. Located in the city are nine other Presbyterian congregations—affiliated with the United ("northern") Presbyterian Church in the U.S.A. A number of the latter are predominantly Negro in membership.[2] The nine hundred

109

members of the Meadowview church are mostly business and sales people occupationally, mostly southern in heritage, and isolated residentially and socially from Negro Christians.

James Lowry became pastor of the congregation in 1960. His sense of the "emotional reality" of the Civil Rights Movement, he says, was closely connected with two events in the summer of 1963: the March on Washington and a local Presbyterian church officers' retreat for eighteen Negro elders and ministers and thirteen white elders and ministers. "This retreat grew out of a friendship with the Negro minister of the Peace Presbyterian Church here in our neighborhood. The retreat was set up so that the white men would be a minority. During the discussions, a young Negro elder wondered skeptically whether he would ever live in a just society. That affected me very deeply. Suddenly there were some individuals whom I loved very much whose lives were hindered and kept down just because they were Negroes. It became very important to me that Negroes in general, and these friends in particular, have the same freedom I had. I began to understand what the word 'involvement' meant."

Soon afterward, he witnessed the March on Washington via television, as recorded in the sermon below. After the sermon at least several members of the congregation took up the challenge of writing to their congressmen in support of the then-pending Civil Rights Bill. Though some objections were voiced, says Mr. Lowry, "four people requested me to meet with them to see what they could do in the area of race relations. Out of that meeting came a desire to meet with members of the Peace Church, and we have been doing this on a monthly basis for a year now with about 25 persons. The Mayor's Commission on Human Rights has asked us to write a pamphlet about this experience. Moreover, because unfair housing practices are probably Louisville's outstanding racial problem, our Women of the Church are planning a Seminar on Democracy in Housing in the spring of 1965. Through sessional committees and other church channels we are trying to communicate with people across the lines of race and class. We cannot have an integrated church until we have an integrated community."

TEXT: ISAIAH 11:6-9

Eleven days ago, in Washington, D.C., there was a signal event. Perhaps it was more than an event. Perhaps it was a sacramental act, a symbolic moment. Call it what you will, it occurred, and it may have an eternal quality about it. Nearly two hundred thousand Negro and white people raised their collective voices in an orderly and dignified affirmation of human freedom under God.

Here was the largest peaceful voice raised in protest against injustice in our day—perhaps in the whole history of mankind. I watched part of it on television. As I watched, the Negro girl who works for us one day a week was in the room. I must confess to strangely mixed feelings. Tears came in my eyes when I heard Marian Anderson sing "He's Got the Whole World in His Hands." They were tears of joy and pride, because I was proud—proud to be a member of the human race. Yet, there were tears of shame. I was ashamed to be a part of a race that made demonstrations like this necessary. I was shamed for my own personal part in this corporate guilt.

Soon afterwards, I read a syndicated article regarding the Washington demonstration. Said this columnist: "The effect of this demonstration was not really in the hands now of the politicians. Rather, it was in the hands of the churches and the synagogues." He indicated that a ground swell of deep feeling from people in the Judaic-Christian tradition would have real effect in moving our lawmakers toward positive legislation. Apathy on the part of the church at this time would lessen the effect of the demonstration.

Certainly this is the time for a rising swell of protest from the Christian community against certain unjust traditions in our society. Certainly this is the time for a rising wave of protest, not from the clergy, but from the grass roots of the church. Those of us in the church are being asked to do more than pray. I would like to urge you to write our representatives in Congress, urging them to vote for a strong Civil Rights legislation.

I do not want this construed as a partisan political statement. This is not an endorsement of a political platform. It is an affirmation of the freedom and dignity of men created in the image of God. I am a registered, and voting, Republican of recent conversion, and this is not with me personally a political issue so much as it is a moral, spiritual, and social issue. This is the time when silence from the church means that we agree with the situation regarding employment practices, and housing practices, and practices in public places throughout our country. This is the time when our silence means that we agree with the philosophy that a man should not have the opportunity for vocational fulfillment simply because of the color of his skin. I therefore would like to urge you, as a member of the Body of Christ, to let the voice of the Christian community, which under God has always been the conscience of the state, ring out loud and clear in these days.

To be sure, if the church moves in this matter now from the grass roots, we will but be jumping on a bandwagon begun by other powers. And if political opportunists and dedicated Communists have prompted this (as I hear people say these days), then they have done from unchristian motivation what the Christian community has failed to do out of love for God and man. And in this way, both politicians and the Communist party are instruments of God's judgment on the Christian community. The Christian's primary question is not what someone else does about a matter, but what he himself, as a Christian, must do about it. The point of concern is not the possible ingratitude of the Negro, or the political ambitions of Kennedy, or the world-wide desire for conquest by Khrushchev. The point of concern is—am I as a Christian committed to work for social justice in a world of injustice? It is not the action of the enemy that concerns the Christian—but what his own action under God will be!

The church discovers herself now in the position of being able to influence the swing of history. And if her people can now rise to the occasion and let their individual and collective voices be heard by the lawmakers and others who guide the destinies of our communities, God may use her in a marvelous way in our day.

In the Christian community a man honestly wants to live in a just society. He works when and where he can for the redemption of his society. He works for a society where men are permitted vocational fulfillment and the right to live and worship where they wish. These rights are not granted by men. They are granted by God. Again I would urge you to make your affirmation of justice known by writing to our representatives in Washington.

Now I am aware that some of you may feel I am saying this because I am a minister. "If you lived in the world we live in, you would not be so ready to say it!" You know, I used to resent that remark, because I probably resented being a minister. But now I feel somewhat differently about it. Now I know this is one of the functions of the Christian ministry, to remind men that there is a world above the world in which all of us live, and that it is a most real world, more real than the one in which we do most of our living, more real because it endures, and the world in which we do most of our living does not endure. So I can say, yes, I am a minister. You called me in good faith, expecting me to say things like this, and to remind you that the Kingdom of God stands above the world in which we live, that the ideal to which I point you stands in judgment over the shallowness of our lives, that the kingdom of love stands in judgment over our kingdom of self-interest, that the kingdom of grace stands in judgment over our kingdom of pride and vanity. So I am not ashamed to say this to you as a minister, nor do I resent being told that I say it because I am a minister. I admit to being an idealist. I feel no sense of accomplishment, or achievement, at this. For what I see and hear and dream I have not gotten. It has been given.

Even as Martin Luther King had a dream, so I have one, too. In this dream I see a time when men will no longer be cursed, imprisoned, and denied by the world because they are the accidents of birth. Men with real wealth will give without snobbery, without fear, and without contempt; and men who are poor will receive these gifts with boundless gratitude, without contempt for themselves or for the one who gave. Men's lives will not be divided into one area of work and one of worship, but men will see every moment as a sacred moment, and every event in their lives, in worship or in work, as a sacramental moment. Men will hunger for the Word of God and for God himself as they now hunger for bread and for things. The people of God will be the people of God and not slaves to this age and its drives and traditions. Men will live in harmony because they love one another, and not because they are afraid of one another. I have such a dream. It is the fulfillment of our Lord's command, "Be ye therefore perfect, even as your Father which is in heaven is perfect."[3]

I do not expect this dream to come true fully in this life. I know it cannot. Once I believed it could. I no longer believe so. But I know it *will* come true, for it is eternal and permanent, and nothing else is. So I am not reluctant to point you to that dream, though I know none of you will ever see its fulfillment in this life. And yet the nature of the dream is such that to realize the impossibility of its fulfillment does not fill one with the sense of utter frustration, but rather with a sense of deepest peace.

I want this dream to haunt you, even as it haunts me. I want it to call you, even as it calls me. I want you to be saddened by the realization that we cannot let it come true, that we will not let it come true, even as I am saddened by that realization. I want it to move you through your daily life as it moves me. I want it to judge your failures as it judges mine. I want the bell of freedom in that dream to ring in your ears and never stop. I want you to hear that bell wherever you sit with your family at table. I want you to hear it in this sanctuary. I want it to ring the loudest in your ears when you are at your shop or office, or traveling in your car, or at your club. I want you to know that when you deny its existence and scoff at it, the bell will ring with a heightened intensity. I want you to know that if you run from it, its peals will follow you down the darkened ways of your mind and heart as it follows me. I want you to give yourself to it and find the adventure, the struggle, the tears, and the joy it gives. And above all, every day of your life, I want you to know that dream is there, above you, around you, and in you—as I know it is above, around, and in me. I want you to know it is your judgment as I know it is mine. I want you to know it is your hope, even as I know it is mine. I want it to free you from the hold this age has on you and that you have on this age.

The prophet Isaiah had this dream. He said, "The wolf shall dwell with the lamb, and the leopard shall lie down with the kid . . . They shall not hurt or destroy in all my holy mountain; for the earth shall be full of the knowledge of the Lord as the waters cover the sea." This is the dream of the prophet, the dream of Christ, the dream of the church. And we are called to raise the voice of affirmation and protest against this age which denies to men what God gives them in this dream.

# Capitulation to Caesar

Jefferson P. Rogers
The Church of the Redeemer, Washington, D.C.
January 19, 1964

The Church of the Redeemer is one of three southern Presbyterian congregations in the nation's capital. Founded in 1958 as a "home mission" effort of Potomac Presbytery, the congregation is predominantly Negro and draws its members chiefly from a middle-class neighborhood in northeastern Washington. Since 1958 its only pastor has been Jefferson P. Rogers.

The congregation has committed itself to becoming "A Fellowship Without Barriers." This intention has been expressed in the large number of congregational programs in which white members of nearby Washington churches have participated—especially an annual series of forums led by the national leaders of the Civil Rights Movement. It has also been expressed by the exceptionally high percentage of members who have participated both in the Civil Rights Movement and in all organizational levels of the southern Presbyterian church. For its size (140 members) this congregation has thus already played an exceptional part in helping to fill the vacuum described above.[1]

Mr. Rogers, who was born and educated chiefly in Florida, states his philosophy of churchmanship as follows: "Practically all areas of our congregation's life have participants who are not Negroes, but we make no fetish of this. Our position is that any Christian church evangelizes among any of the members of the human race. We do not observe Race Relations Sunday at all. It militates against the logic of our very existence."

On grounds of such a position, Mr. Rogers believes that the Church of the Redeemer has a long-term mission not only to combat racist attitudes but also to combat class attitudes associated with both the Negro middle class and American Presbyterianism. In a publication distributed to the congregation he writes: "Neither Malcolm X, nor any other person similar to him in background, could have been rescued by a typical Presbyterian church from the social abyss of dope users and penitentiary life. Our guilt is further compounded because we feel no conscious guilt about this neglect as we strive to find a seat at the table of the affluent. . . . We must organize our love to reach out to the oppressed who are candidates for the therapy of the justified hatred so admirably fashioned by Elijah Muhammed and company," while at the same time, he adds, combatting the pride and prejudice of the white segregationist.[2]

Political exploitation of class and racist attitudes within the Negro community itself is the provocation of the sermon printed below. As a Federal District, Washington is governed by a Board of Commissioners whose members are nominated by the President of the United States and approved by the U.S. Senate. In mid-1963 one of the incumbent commissioners declined reappointment to the board by President Kennedy in the light of certain income tax and other financial delinquencies which had been made public. Local leaders of the Democratic party then campaigned for the nomination of a former local president of the NAACP, a Negro minister who had also been elected recently to the National Democratic Committee. It was publicly known, reports Mr. Rogers, that this politically active minister "had absconded with funds during his reign as local NAACP president. All this amounted to an atmosphere unbecoming to the Christian church as well as to a reflection on the Negro community. What progress had we made when such a person was regarded (however falsely) as representative of the church in the Negro community?"

Politically speaking, the sermon below was not "successful"; the former NAACP president was soon after appointed to the District Board of Commissioners. But it called the attention of a predominantly Negro congregation to a substratum of the Civil Rights Movement which both minorities and majorities will be tempted to forget in the post-1964 era: Whether expressed crudely in the purchase of Negro votes or sophisticatedly in the nominating of Negro candidates, racism is irrelevant to democratic politics; and democracy needs a politically unencumbered church to keep democracy well reminded of this principle.

TEXT: JEREMIAH 5:26-31

Benjamin Mays stood before an auditorium packed with students who would have been present even if attendance had not been compulsory. He was speaking to young people, and his major concern was about their morale. He knew that all of us lived in a culture determined to eliminate high aspiration in Negroes before it could become deeply rooted in them. Dr. Mays said that if he had to choose between being loved or respected, he would choose respect. I cannot remember his argument in detail, but it included the contention that one cannot truly love what he does not respect. Since southern white people made such an insistent point regarding their alleged love for Negroes, Dr. Mays was concerned to point out the meaninglessness of any love which demanded a background of utter disrespect. He was insisting that the student become the gardener of his own respect, both from others and from himself.

I am reminded of two examples of such disrespect. In that same auditorium, Dr. William Gray, then president of Florida A. & M. College, told his students in the presence of local whites, segregated in the best seats in the auditorium during a vesper service in 1948, that it was foolhardy for Negroes to think that they were as good and as able as the white students who attended the companion white university at Gainesville, Florida. Here was a Philadelphia-born Negro, with a Ph.D. from the University of Pennsylvania, instructing his students, through boos and catcalls, that they were foolhardy and lazy to spend their time on civil rights when it was obvious that they were no match for their white companions. The other occasion was earlier. In 1944 the Republican party of Philadelphia sent all of the Negro A.M.E. churches checks amounting to $75.00 or more the Sunday *before* the election. The common denominator in both instances was disrespect so complete that subtlety was not thought necessary. Disrespect in any form is bad enough, but here its objects were expected not only not to recognize such gestures as disrespectful, but to be grateful for being discounted.

In each of these instances the regard for whites was categorically opposite to the regard for Negroes. That such disrespect could be duplicated on many other occasions in American life did not lessen its ugliness to me, nor mitigate the inward sense of revulsion which I experienced on witnessing the two incidents. The roots of disrespect are indeed deep. Perhaps it was less the disrespect in our culture that provoked nausea in me, than, rather, that the pivot for its execution in each instance was a Negro. In one case a college president, in the other a bishop. One source of disrespect originated from without, the other from within. Dr. Mays' words once more seared themselves in my brain: If I have to choose between being loved and respected, I would rather be respected.

It is primarily respect for the institution of the church on the one hand and integrity of race on the other that are involved in a third occasion facing us this morning. This occasion gives me the unavoidable responsibility of outlining for members of the Church of the Redeemer the Christian doctrine of church and state.

In brief, the situation is this: It is possible that we, as citizens of the District of Columbia, will be confronted with the option of voting for or against a local Negro pastor for office as a partisan official in a major political party. We will be asked to do so as Christians and as Negroes. There is a brazenness in this request which is rooted squarely in the history of the disrespect about which we have been thinking together thus far. First of all, the brazenness is encouched in the understandable belief that no Negro clergyman would publicly speak to an issue involving another Negro clergyman. The other is that no white clergyman would be likely to do so because of the fear of being regarded as prejudiced. And the very silence of the white pulpit on this issue is mute testimony to the carefully taught disrespect for Negro institutions. Thus this is careful, skillful brazenness.

Americans fear the powerful, successful man. Power is license in modern societies, and Caesar is king, even amongst church people. We are afraid both of established power and of potential power. This fear, this weakness, is not a racial but a cultural characteristic. When Commodore Vanderbilt was once reminded of what the law indicated he could not do in the building of his steamship empire, his reply was: "I got the power, ain't I?" On a more recent occasion when I reminded Chuck Stone, then of *The Afro-American,* of the attack on the NAACP by Adam Clayton Powell, he replied, "But he got 100,000 votes in Harlem." This potential fear of success is present in the brazenness about which I speak. As a matter of fact, it was used in intimidation processes to get sponsors for the would-be candidate, if the testimony of several people is accurate.

There is at least one important parallel in this present experience with that of the other two instances cited. It is only the *Negro* community from which a *clergyman* is being presented as an adequate representative of the church and the state. There is not one white clergyman of any significant repute who would run for a national office in either of the major parties. He would not dare propose it to his constituency. Would Dr. Elson, Dr. Docherty, Dr. Cranford, Bishop O'Boyle, Dr. Colwell, or Dr. John Randolph Taylor become candidates for elected political office on this level? Would Mr. Rauh, self-styled mayor of Negroes in Washington, appeal to a Jewish rabbi whom he would thereby expect to feel flattered by the opportunity to be endorsed by others selected by the Central Democratic Committee? The answer is the same answer that would do justice to the occasion on which the Republican party sent checks to Negro churches in Philadelphia, which was for the simple reason that they not only did not respect the churches in question, but were confident that the churches did not respect themselves enough to return the money with proper ecclesiastical cussing. Mr. Rauh's cynical use of the Negro community through the willingness of a Negro pastor who winks at the integrity of the church and the traditional low regard for Negro competence is the essence of disrespect. In the name of the church we must cry out against it, and remind ourselves what the church of the living God is when it is the church.

This means, first of all, that it is a community above race, as we remind ourselves every morning in our service of worship. This is not simply an isolated fact, irrelevant to the development of our society. It means that the focus is always on the adequacy of the individual and not on his color. I do not fear being represented by a man who happens to be white. My concern is what kind of man is he otherwise. John F. Kennedy was white, but otherwise, the salt of the earth! As we think about the defects of this land, we ought to be impressed with our need to develop cultural power and affluence which will eliminate undeserved penalty for those who are of the minority. But we must not insist on the right to have our proper quota of scoundrels also! Our qualitative need is to rid ourselves of scoundrels of any hue at the same time that we widen the horizon of opportunity for all. I would be as delighted to have Ralph Bunche as President of the United States as I was to have been a citizen under John Fitzgerald Kennedy, and for the same reason. Let us remember this, both as democratic citizens and as Christians. Let us see to it that no right-thinking person who happens to be white will have anything to fear from us. Let us be able enough to prevent any chicanerous person from trading his whiteness for support which he does not merit on the basis of pertinent standards. Let us also be realistic enough to know that we need cultural power to deal with both white and black folk, for we must remember that this is the church of Christ and that its spiritual and cultural health should attract people who love God, and who want to create a society in keeping with what God demands.

Our nation and the world need the church to be the church. The separation of the church from political machinery of the state is as much for the good of the state as for the integrity of the church. Karl Barth, who has lived through a society shaken to its foundations by malevolent Caesars, tells us,

The Church must remain the Church. It must remain the inner circle of the Kingdom of Christ. The Christian community has a task of which the civil community can never relieve it and which it can never pursue in the forms peculiar to the civil community. . . . It proclaims the rule of Jesus Christ and the hope of the Kingdom of God. This is not the task of the civil community: it has no message to deliver; it is dependent on a message being delivered to it. It is not in a position to appeal to the authority and grace of God; it is dependent on this happening elsewhere. It does not pray; it depends on others praying for it. It is blind to the Whence? and Whither? of human existence . . . it depends on the existence of seeing eyes elsewhere. . . . The thought and speech of the civil community wavers necessarily between a much too childlike optimism and a much too peevish pessimism in regard to man—as a matter of course it expects the best of everybody and suspects the worst! It obviously relies on its own view of man being fundamentally superseded elsewhere.[3]

If the voice of the head of the church is also the voice of a political machine, necessarily involved in chicanery, what happens to the will of God as the leaven of the social loaf? What happens when the messenger of God takes orders from, rather than serves as a corrective to, Caesar? What happens when one sees the vestments of God and hears the voice of Caesar?

Let no worshiper here misunderstand me to be saying the church should be unconcerned with and not involved in issues that are directly concerned with politics. To the contrary, all the major political issues require immense concern on the part of the church. The church must guard against greed and against the corruption that always results from uninhibited power; and to buy off the protector, to pollute the watchman, is always the aim of those who would steal the city. The prophet Jeremiah dealt heavily with these very issues. His cry was a cry which could only come from one whose roots were unmistakably those of the prophetic clergyman:

" 'For wicked men are found among my people;
    they lurk like fowlers lying in wait.
They set a trap;
    they catch men.
Like a basket full of birds,
    their houses are full of treachery;
therefore they have become great and rich,
    they have grown fat and sleek.
They know no bounds in deeds of wickedness;
    they judge not with justice

the cause of the fatherless, to make it prosper,
   and they do not defend the rights of the needy.
Shall I not punish them for these things?
                          says the LORD,
   and shall I not avenge myself
   on a nation such as this?'


"An appalling and horrible thing
   has happened in the land:
the prophets prophesy falsely,
   and the priests rule at their direction;
my people love to have it so,
   but what will you do when the end comes?"
                          (Jeremiah 5:26-31).


Now it is all but inevitable that someone will object that public criticism of Washington politicians ought to be withheld because their public image may be impaired. Someone may also say, as it was said in the day of Jeremiah, "my people love to have it so." But I remind you that the choice is one involving respect or disrespect. Always, the history of our nation bears out, always it is the Negro community which is expected to absorb the insults and to suffer in comparison with the other communities in our pluralistic society. I remind you that respect which does not become established from within cannot be effected from without. Therefore the price of silence on matters this crucial is an open acceptance of disrespect which would not be tolerated by other communities. To protect men against the institutionalized hate that degrades them with or without the consent of their leaders is the political concern of the church. Caesar is Caesar because he has temporary power. The church is the church because it will not permit that power to be effective in the relationship between Caesar and the church. Yes, Caesar has the power to make the church suffer, but he does not have the power to make the church not the church while men still believe in God. Our doctrine must be that when the church refuses to suffer and seeks chiefly to avoid suffering, it ceases thereby to be the church. Suffering is the inevitable lot of him who guards the gates to the golden city.

As Christians, we must remember that the word we bring against others is the same word we bring against ourselves. Harry Ashmore once gave advice to white southerners which we might well profit from today. He suggested that *"no people have ever prospered by exalting their fools and driving off their prophets."* His "epitaph for Dixie" was, *"the tragedy lies not in the battles we lost, but in the battles we never fought."*[4]

We must repudiate the counsel to support the ambitions of a Caesar who walks where the prophet should hold forth. We must fight this fight because no one else can fight it for us. If we do not fight it, we deserve to stand alone as the only people who can be cynically used in a day when other groups need to see our integrity and intelligence flying at full mast. You can choose between respect and sentimentality. You can render unto God the things that are God's; you can find the strength, even when Caesar is victorious, not to be among those whose strategy is capitulation to Caesar.

# The Maker of Peace

D. P. McGeachy III
First Presbyterian Church, Gainesville, Georgia
June 28, 1964

Gainesville is the county seat of Hall County, fifty miles northeast of Atlanta, on Lake Sidney Lanier. Its architecture is a combination of antebellum columns and ranch-modern, indicative of growing pains in the last two decades. The town's economy depends chiefly upon textile mills, poultry processing plants, and the presence of Brenau College and Riverside Military Academy. The population is approximately 18,000.

"About four thousand of us are Negroes," says Mr. McGeachy, in a use of the pronoun which suggests what the Civil Rights struggle has been all about. Pastor of the First Presbyterian Church (membership 650) since 1959, he was appointed in the spring of 1964 to the local mayor's committee on race relations. Though most Gainesville Negroes live in substandard housing and job opportunities for them are very limited, a massive urban renewal program has just begun, and local firms are moving toward more democratic hiring practices. For a number of years Negroes have been serving in key positions such as the school board, the police force, the probation office, and the mayor's advisory committee on housing. In 1962 the Chattahoochee Country Club was integrated without incident.

"Because of this progress," says Mr. McGeachy, "little disturbance was expected in 1964 with the passage of the Civil Rights Act. As the time drew close, however, certain undercurrents of hostility stirred in the community, and the mayor's committee suddenly became active after several months of not meeting. The committee organized three subcommittees: Job Opportunities, Public Accommodations, and Churches. The first has the most difficult task, and as yet has little to report. The Churches subcommittee has discovered that almost all of the churches in Gainesville have plans to seat any Negroes who may wish to worship. At first the Public Accommodations subcommittee had a ruckus on their hands when a fight broke out in an attempt to integrate the local pool hall on the Monday after the law was signed. Some rock-throwing, a few arrests, and a couple of days of police curfews followed, but the mayor's committee was able to negotiate a peace rather easily.

"Today almost all accommodations are open, including the drug store counter mentioned in the sermon. On the surface we are a law-abiding community with continued 'good relations.' As the sermon tries to indicate, however, there are 'miles to go before we sleep.' "

## TEXT: EPHESIANS 2:11-22

"Something there is that doesn't love a wall . . ."[1]

One of the empirical proofs of the inspiration of the Christian Scripture is its ability to touch the heartstrings. There are passages that send the spirit bubbling with irresistible joy or infect it with the rhythm of victorious marching. And there are those that stimulate a catch in the throat, a sob, or a spasm of guilt. One that speaks most movingly to the tenor of our times, both in its sadness and its hope, is Ephesians 2:12-14.

> "Remember that you were . . . separated from Christ, alienated from the commonwealth of Israel, and strangers to the covenants of promise, having no hope and without God in the world. But now in Christ Jesus you who once were far off have been brought near in the blood of Christ. For he is our peace, who has made us both one, and has broken down the dividing wall of hostility."

That first sentence is the saddest in all of literature. It transcends in pathos Whittier's haunting phrase: "It might have been!"[2] It is even more chilling than Milton's tragic line about Samson's downfall: "Eyeless in Gaza, at the mill with slaves."[3] For beyond pain and death, ignorance and frustration, man's chief enemies are hopelessness, loneliness, and separation.

Paul is referring to the division existing between the people of God and the nations of man. Although her mission was to the

Gentiles, Israel used her chosenness to remain aloof from the world. And in Paul's day, misunderstanding existed within the church between those who had grown up in the orthodox Hebrew tradition and those who had come from a Gentile background. This was the most important "dividing wall" troubling the early church. As time has passed, other divisions have loomed large on the human scene, like that which caused the schism of the Reformation. As this has happened, Ephesians 2:12-14 has flashed from many facets, like a gem growing richer with age. Today it continues to cast light on the principal divisions that separate us from one another and from God.

Every age knows the meaning of loneliness, for it is the principal by-product of human sin. The twentieth century is no exception. Hostility is present in larger and smaller amounts in the lives of people. It is apparent in the cleavage that causes children and parents, though they hunger for one another, to go away empty, each speaking his own language. We observe it in the inability of those who love each other dearly to communicate their heart's longings. Loneliness hangs heavy over the newest dormitory on the campus of the University of Georgia, a building housing one thousand freshman girls, each wondering in the midst of the crowd where to find a kindred heart and a friendly hand. Some of us are more aggressive than others; we reach out the glad hand and assert our friendship, but within us all, someone has said, is a "wallflower heart."

Consider Willy Loman, the salesman who dies desperately trying to convince himself that he is a success, but knowing that in the eyes of all those whose respect he cherishes he is an incompetent.[4] Consider the employer who makes decisions that drastically affect the lives of his workers, but who cannot speak with them about it; or the worker who sits endlessly at his monotonous duty and dreams, not of creativity or of world abuilding, but of next weekend or the promise of a five-hour day. Consider the elderly man, still vital in body and mind, forcefully retired from his chosen profession and living out his years in uselessness. All such hapless souls, strangers to the covenants of promise, are cut off from one another, and so from God.

In the midst of this fragmented mess, the tension between people of different races is the most obvious and painful of our separations. In small ways we brush against one another and the little sparks fly. In Gainesville last week, two men who work in the same business establishment went into a drugstore for lunch. The man whose skin was white said to the counterman, "A hot dog, please."

The counterman turned and bawled to the short-order cook: "One dog!"

Then the man whose skin was black said to the counterman, "I'll have the same, please."

And the counterman bawled to the kitchen, "One dog *to go!*"

A small thing, but one of the stones out of which a great wall is constructed—a dividing wall of hostility.

Both the cause and the result of this wall's existence can be found in the ominous words of our text: "Without God in the world." When there is no vertical relationship there can be none that is horizontal; if I do not love God with all my being, then I cannot love my neighbor as myself. And the converse is true: if I hate my brother, then I am a liar if I say I love God (1 John 4:20). Thus the solution to the dilemma does not lie in the legislation of Congress or the decisions of the courts. It is to be found in the changing of men's hearts. So wrote one of our state legislators: "I have concluded that the answer will only be found when the people of Georgia find it upon their knees." And at the same time, we must not suppose that prayer is confined to direct address. That which we do and say in our daily relationships with one another is a legitimate worship. The senator could have written: "The people of Georgia will never really kneel until they have first gone and made peace with their brethren."

Separation from God cuts us off from man because it destroys our hope. Every schoolboy in Greece memorized the hopeless words of Oedipus the king:

"Not to be born is past all prizing best; but when a man has seen the light, this is next best by far: that with all speed he should go thither whence he hath come."[5]

And when this Greek pessimism touched the Old Testament, Ecclesiastes sang:

> "What has been is what will be,
>    and what has been done is what will be done;
>    and there is nothing new under the sun" (1:9).

Not to believe in the possibility of Christ and his resurrection is thus to give up and long for death. It is to say, "There's no use trying." But to hear the words of Paul, "For by grace you have been saved through faith; and this is not your own doing, it is the gift of God" (Ephesians 2:8), is to be set free from the fear of failure and the futility of hopelessness.

There really is no such thing as separation from God.

> "If I make my bed in Sheol, thou art there!
> If I take the wings of the morning
>    and dwell in the uttermost parts of the sea,
> even there thy hand shall lead me" (Psalm 139:8-10).

This means that the "dividing wall of hostility" is erected by *us*, to wall God out. His eternal invitation, "Whoever will, let him come," is a standing one. He accepts us as we are, "while we are yet sinners," and offers us peace.

Once we have been freed from preoccupation with being god to ourselves we can receive the peace which he offers. Then, having our own lives "hid with Christ in God," we are free to be the instruments of that acceptance in the world. We can become "no longer strangers and sojourners, but . . . fellow citizens with the saints and members of the household of God" (Ephesians 2:19). As such, our duty is clear: both to live and to tell the gospel of peace "that through the church the manifold wisdom of God might . . . be made known" to the universe (Ephesians 3:10). And that wisdom also is obvious,

> "For he has made known to us . . . the mystery of his will . . .
> to unite all things in him, things in heaven and things on
> earth" (Ephesians 1:9-10).

Let's translate this theology into the terms of everyday experience. So long as I am worried about what other people think of me, I am unable to be a very nice person. I am too busy trying to be clever, or cute, or important. I have to show by my money, my position, or my fancy behavior that I am somebody the world ought to notice. If, however, I can be released from this self-preoccupation, I can concentrate on other people and their needs. In order to have friends, I must be a friend.

But how do I find this release? It comes to me in the form of love and acceptance from my parents, my friends, my church, as they mediate the love of God to me. If I know that I am accepted, I am free to accept others. This is what Jesus meant in saying that life is to be found in losing it.

It follows then that the church, being the people who know themselves to belong securely to God, is the instrument to mediate this security to others. Of all people, we who know that we are sinners forgiven by God ought to be free from the need to look down upon others. Prejudice, it is said, is rooted in man's desire to be important. Because of this he finds false importance in calling another man his inferior. But we have all the importance that could ever be sought: we have been made sons of God. Thus we belie our heritage of faith when we downgrade our neighbor.

All this means something very practical when it comes to our responsibility under the laws of our land. As the Civil Rights Bill is signed, there are three possible reactions to it.

The first is to defy it, like Pickrick.[6] It goes without saying that law-abiding citizens under God reject such behavior.

The second is to say, "Well, I don't like it, but I will obey it if it is the law." Perhaps this is a shade better.

But there is a third response, demanded by our theology. That is to take this civil action and to baptize it: to use it as a God-given vehicle for saying louder what we have been saying all along, or to say at last what we have not dared yet to say: that God in Christ has made all men his children for his own glory and for our peace.

We began with the loneliness of verse 12; we must conclude with the warm rejoicing of the rest of the text:

"But now in Christ Jesus you who once were far off have been brought near in the blood of Christ. For he is our peace, who has made us both one, and has broken down the dividing wall of hostility."

When the angels heralded his birth, they sang of this peace. To his disciples in the upper room he left this legacy, giving them a peace "not of this world." It is not a peace casually apprehended; it may seem more like a sword than anything else, for it must cut away at the infected areas of our lives and such surgery involves pain. But it is a peace worth the price. It is "peace with God through our Lord Jesus Christ."

The dividing wall of hostility is down; it remains for us simply to walk through the breach. From the rubble of that separation there is a new structure being erected,

"built upon the foundation of the apostles and prophets, Christ Jesus himself being the cornerstone, in whom the whole structure is joined together and grows into a holy temple in the Lord; in whom you also are built into it for a dwelling place of God in the Spirit."

# God's Agents

Paul Tudor Jones
Idlewild Presbyterian Church, Memphis, Tennessee
September 6, 1964

Now a city of half a million, Memphis, Tennessee, is the longtime capital of the Cotton Kingdom. Financially supported by the cotton economy, it has shaped and been shaped by the traditions and customs of the entire Mid-South cotton-growing area. The population is forty-two percent Negro.

Memphis has been desegregating its public facilities quietly and without violence for a number of years, but especially since the meeting of the Memphis Community Relations Committee with the Mayor and Board of Commissioners on March 25, 1960. Before the Civil Rights Act of 1964, Memphis had desegregated its major hotels, motels, restaurants, theaters, libraries, parks and playgrounds, city bus system, public schools, and civic auditorium. Some progress has also been made toward removing discriminatory restrictions from employment in Memphis business and industry. "There are many factors in peaceful desegregation of the city," says Dr. Jones. "We are fortunate to have a large number of registered Negro voters (93,000) who have taken part in the city's political life for many years, very capable Negro leaders, a police system which enforces the law efficiently and justly, and Civil Rights organizations which are both aggressive and cooperative."

The Idlewild Presbyterian Church has a membership of two thousand persons, drawn from many sectors of the city and representing a fair cross section of business, professional, and social life in the white segment of the population. Many of the lay leaders in the congregation have been participants in the movement for peaceful desegregation of the city's community life.

131

The sermon, "God's Agents," was preached on September 6, 1964, at a time when criticism was running high throughout the Mid-South because of the activities of the National Council of Churches. Movements were on foot in many congregations of various denominations to force withdrawal from the National Council of Churches. Some southern Presbyterian congregations and even a few presbyteries in the General Assembly had declared their intention to cut off all benevolent contributions which might in any way support the work of the Council. Criticism of the Council stemmed principally from its role in training the college students who participated in the 1964 Mississippi Delta Project of the Congress of Federated Organizations (COFO). "The prevailing idea most frequently encountered," reports Dr. Jones, "went something like this: 'Civil rights is a political matter; the church has no business meddling in politics; the church's mission is to save souls; the National Council should stay out of what doesn't concern it.' So this sermon was preached in an attempt to furnish facts where there seemed to be much misunderstanding and to interpret the mission of the church in terms of the ministry of reconciliation. Reaction to the sermon was quite sharply divided, but most people seemed grateful for new information and for the correlation of contemporary social action with Scripture and the traditional ministry of the church. When *The Presbyterian Outlook* later reprinted the sermon, I received from all over the General Assembly expressions of agreement with this point of view."[1]

## TEXT: LUKE 6:46

Many faithful church members in recent weeks have asked me questions about the National Council of Churches. "Are we, Presbyterians, in the National Council?" they ask. "Is it true that the National Council is responsible for this Mississippi Summer Project which has stirred up so much trouble? How much money do we at Idlewild give to the National Council of Churches?"

When I have tried to answer such questions or to help people get hold of the information they are seeking from reliable sources, in many instances the dilemma of these faithful people instead of being resolved has been rather worse confounded.

For example, the question: "Is the National Council responsible for the Mississippi Summer Project?" Investigation reveals that the National Council of Churches did not originate the Mississippi

Summer Project; that it does not sponsor it; that it "did *not* recruit the 450 student volunteers now conducting literacy and voter education classes in Mississippi," and "has no control over policy, strategy, rationale or personnel in the Summer Project"[2]—and that all this is done by a coordination of such organizations as CORE, SNCC, and NAACP. Investigation also reveals that the National Council of Churches did offer to set up training schools for the volunteers and equip them with knowledge, attitudes, and techniques for carrying out this project. At this, many of my interrogators have said: "This is just as bad, if not worse."

Investigation of National Council of Churches financing shows that our whole denomination gives to N.C.C. annually just $8,000. Idlewild Church's share in this for 1964 will be a little less than $50.00. But not one cent of southern Presbyterian money has gone into the financing of the N.C.C. part in the Mississippi Summer Project. That program has been financed entirely by voluntary contributions given for that specific project by individuals and denominations who elected to participate. Our southern Presbyterian church did not elect to participate.

The facts concerning our membership in the Council are equally disquieting to some. The N.C.C. is not a super church, in which individuals or local congregations hold membership. It is "a Council of Churches" or denominations. Membership is through denominational affiliation. Our General Assembly votes to belong or to get out. There is no such thing as an individual or a congregation joining or getting out of the Council. It has been upsetting to many people that they cannot register their protest about the Council's activity by withholding funds (since they do not give) nor by getting out (since membership is not an individual or congregational affair). So what is to be done?

Let me suggest that our controversy with the National Council of Churches is really symptomatic of a deeper concern. We aren't getting the help we need on this problem because we aren't asking the right questions. Here are the real questions we need to ask:

(1) What is the mission of the church of Jesus Christ in the world?

(2) Who is doing God's work in the world today?

(3) Is the church? Am I? If the church and I are not doing his work and others are, what should be my attitude toward whomever God uses as his agents?

The Gospel of Luke records in the fourth chapter the launching of Jesus' Galilean ministry. On the Sabbath he went into the synagogue at Nazareth, where he had been brought up. He was invited to read the lesson from the prophets. He chose Isaiah 61: 1-2: "The Spirit of the Lord is upon me, because he hath anointed me to preach the gospel to the poor; he hath sent me to heal the brokenhearted, to preach deliverance to the captives, and recovering of sight to the blind, to set at liberty them that are bruised, to preach the acceptable year of the Lord" (Luke 4:18-19, K.J.V.). And he closed the scroll and said: "This day is this scripture fulfilled in your ears" (Luke 4:21, K.J.V.).

E. Stanley Jones called this "The Christian Manifesto." The Lord of the church was laying down his platform. The church, when she has been true to her Lord, has taken this manifesto for her marching orders. She has preached the good news of God's grace in Christ to the poor. She has brought healing and help to brokenhearted and hopeless peoples everywhere. She has fought oppression and injustice and in every way effected deliverance of men who were captives of fear, of superstition, of oppressive social, economic, and political systems. She has brought sight to the blind—not only physical sight, but also sight to the spiritually blind who could not recognize the grace of God, and the intellectually blind whose eyes had not been opened to the mysteries of the printed page and the powers of the enlightened mind.

When the now infamous Mississippi Project of CORE, SNCC, SCLC, and the NAACP was launched in June and the 450 young American college students began their work, it was announced that they would engage in a threefold mission:

(1) They would carry on relief work among destitute Negroes —the poorly housed, the ill-fed, the sick; they would bring in and give away clothing and groceries and drugs.

(2) They would teach adult illiterates to read and write. They would organize schools meeting in churches and homes to equip

men and women with this basic skill upon which all development of the best human resources depends.

(3) They would train native-born American Negro citizens how to qualify to vote and assume responsible citizenship.

When this mission began a great cry went up. It has been echoed in the churches: "What is the National Council of Churches thinking about, training workers to engage in such a mission?"

A few years ago the Memphis Rotary Club got interested in the World-Wide Literacy Program of Methodist missionary Frank Laubach and financed and promoted this work which Dr. Laubach has called "opening the eyes of the blind to behold the wonders of the printed page." Memphis became the center of the World Literacy Program that reached out to teach adult illiterates in Africa and Asia—and even Negroes in Shelby County, using the facilities of our Educational TV station WKNO. And nobody damned the Rotary Club or threatened to withdraw membership or withhold financial support. Indeed, the Memphis Rotary Club received nationwide acclaim for this humanitarian project.

The Memphis Public Transit System has for some time been making available a hall where volunteer white workers could teach illiterate adult Negroes to read and write. Nobody has burned down the building or bombed the hall or threatened the lives of the teachers—but over two dozen Negro churches in Mississippi have been burned or bombed this summer because in some instances they have been used for meeting places to carry on adult education.

For years we have been collecting old clothes and blankets and food and drugs in our Memphis churches and sending them as relief supplies to destitute people all over the world through Church World Service (a branch of the National Council of Churches), and most of us have thought we were obeying Christ's command: "Inasmuch as ye have done it unto one of the least of these my brethren, ye have done it unto me" (Matthew 25:40, K.J.V.).

Similarly, the Memphis Shelby County Red Cross Chapter is gathering used clothing to meet the emergency needs of families

who may be burned out of their homes this coming winter. No one
has sworn out a warrant for the arrest of the Red Cross workers or
threatened to withhold contributions of clothing because this is
relief work and some of it might go to Negro families.

When in recent days an energetic young businessman of Memphis called and told me that he and his cohorts in the Shelby
County Republican Association were conducting a voter registration drive and wanted the churches' help with making announce-
ments to urge that people register and vote, I saw no occasion for
getting angry or asking him to leave the church premises.

I may know little about the ideals of organizations such as
CORE, SNCC, SCLC, the NAACP; but these facts are evident
to all:

(1) Under the auspices of these organizations 450 college
young people volunteered to carry on without pay the above-
mentioned threefold mission. They agreed to live in substandard
conditions through their whole vacation time, to support themselves and to carry with them their own bail money in the event
that they were jailed for engaging in such humanitarian relief and
educational work.

(2) These young people have followed a non-violent approach
in all their endeavors. There has not been a single instance of
assault by one of them, though some of them have been insulted,
beaten, and murdered while on their mission.

When the Sanhedrin in Jerusalem, the official governing body
of the Jewish church, was considering the imposition of further im-
prisonment and punishment of the apostles Peter and John for
their courageous action in carrying on the ministry of Jesus Christ
under painful persecution, Gamaliel, Israel's wise old teacher,
said to his colleagues: "Take heed to yourselves what ye intend to
do as touching these men. . . . Refrain from these men, and let
them alone: for if this counsel or this work be of men, it will come
to nought: but if it be of God, ye cannot overthrow it; lest haply
ye be found even to fight against God" (Acts 5:35, 38-39,
K.J.V.).

For us today, the real question is not: "Am I for or against the
National Council of Churches and its participation in the Missis-

sippi Summer Project?" We have deeper and more serious questions to ponder: "What is the mission of the church of Jesus Christ? Am I actively engaged in that mission? Does my Lord today find me fighting for or against him? What should my attitude be toward those who are performing a Christlike ministry which I refrain from performing?"

# Facing the Truth

Joe S. McClure
Huntersville Presbyterian Church
Huntersville, North Carolina
June 4, 1961

The final four sermons of this collection concern the struggle of certain congregations to embody a raceless gospel in a raceless fellowship in social communities where race is still a stubbornly real standard of human evaluation. In this sense, the concluding sermons do some justice to the southern Presbyterian doctrine of the spirituality of the church. Like all heresies, this one had in it an important truth: the Christian church is called to be something which no other social institution is expected to be.

Huntersville, North Carolina, is a town of about one thousand persons located in Piedmont North Carolina. Just eight miles from Charlotte, it is slowly taking on suburban characteristics. The section enjoys a rich history. The so-called Mecklenburg Declaration of Independence, which pre-dated the national Declaration in Philadelphia, is supposed to have been signed by the Scotch-Irish Presbyterian settlers on a plantation adjacent to Huntersville. The strong Presbyterian heritage in the area has put a high value on integrity and justice.

The Negro community is set apart to the south and east of town and comprises about one third of the population. It has a modern high school and five churches with no full-time pastors. Negro men work chiefly as construction laborers; the women do domestic work in the white community. There had been no serious local racial unrest when this sermon was preached. There was a growing tension, however, heightened by a lack of communication between the two communities.

The Huntersville Presbyterian Church, located in the center of town, is the largest congregation in a "totally churched" community.

In 1961 it had about four hundred members, representing almost every community group except Negroes.

Joe S. McClure was called as pastor of the congregation in July, 1955, after graduation from seminary. References to congregational responsibility in the racial crisis were regularly made in his sermons, and on two Race Relations Sundays in the late fifties he devoted entire sermons to the subject. A year before June 4, 1961, the session had officially established the policies recounted in the sermon below, and at a called meeting before the sermon the policies were reaffirmed by a unanimous vote of those present. Two elders were absent.

"The initial response of the congregation," Mr. McClure remembers, "was a studied silence. Tuesday morning a Charlotte newspaper carried an article which quoted the proposed policies. The results of the article were almost explosive in Huntersville. The subject that no one had been able to talk about was suddenly on everyone's lips. The resulting conversations were a river of confusion, as muddy as the neighboring Catawba, and fed by streams flowing from contradictory springs in the mind of each individual.

"The response within the congregation was almost totally one of deep concern. Most of the church membership contacted me within the first two days to say, 'I just called to say I'm on your side'; and 'I'm glad the church has taken a stand. I can't fully agree with it but I know it's right.' Some of the older folk could only whisper, 'I know you didn't mean it.' These statements were usually followed by confession-like reminiscences of racial injustice which had been eating like a cancer in many a conscience.

"In all, the church seemed to have been strengthened by the occasion. The church had now been the Church. We had demonstrated that the church's house was built on a rock. Contrary to our expectations, attendance and contributions increased.

"The response of the Negro community was much slower. At first there were only warmer smiles and someone crossing the street to shake your hand. Members of our church said that maids who had grown distant in their attitudes were warm and conversant again. A staff member of a local hospital called to say that tensions between the Negro and white personnel had eased. This initial warmth was soon followed by an increased number of invitations to speak at Negro schools and churches. The principal of the Negro high school had previously made overtures to the white community for cooperative leadership in dealing with his school and community problems. This cooperation was given, and in the state program his group won the area award in Community Development with the only integrated presentation in the state.

"As I look back on the situation now, I have the feeling that the 'Bible Belt,' for all its disclaimers, has molded a strong sense of justice and of the sovereignty of God into the consciences of its population. There is an awful agony in the process, but these folk seem to come through with more integrity than they or outsiders may always recognize."

## TEXT: ISAIAH 56:6-8; EPHESIANS 4:1-7

The May 13, 1961, issue of the *Saturday Evening Post* contains an article by Robert Paul Sessions, entitled "Are Southern Ministers Failing the South?" He commends those ministers in the South who have taken the lead in giving sane guidance in the problem of race relations since the Supreme Court decision in 1954. While these men have been accused by some of betraying the South, says he, it is clear to any thinking person that their leadership has been the only thing that has saved us from untold terror.

On the other hand, he accuses the vast majority of ministers in the South of soft-pedaling or ignoring the issue altogether because of their fear of facing up to the truth. I must confess some personal sense of guilt in the matter. Although we as a congregation have not ignored the issue and have dealt forthrightly with it, we have never declared how we stand by clearly announcing our policy, belief, and action.

The time has come for us to face realistically the truth of the situation, to commit ourselves to a policy that is clear and unmistakable. Thus, I propose this morning to give some analyses of the situation in Huntersville, to recommend a policy for our church, and to suggest some practical applications of this policy.

*The Situation.* We as a congregation have enjoyed a role of leadership in this community. We have sought to influence the affairs of the community with wisdom and justice. Regarding the matter of race relations during the past six years, however, we have been able to offer little, if any, leadership, because we have been a divided and confused group. Not divided against each other, but divided and confused within ourselves.

Indeed, the situation has been so confused that we have been able to speak of it only in the most general terms and then only with friends and family. Our conversation has been largely the hope that the situation will "die down" or will wait for the next generation for a solution.

Surprisingly, by looking back we can see that each of us has changed during the past six years. Our initial alarm and disbelief at the Negro's rising shout of protest have turned slowly into a passive acceptance of the situation and a wait-and-see attitude. Our initial indignation has turned into a hope for a just solution.

Each of us has found himself to be two persons, and these two persons have had a hard time living together. One side of us clings to the traditional southern belief that the segregated order was divinely ordained. The other side has all along realized that there is a blind spot in our lives, inherited from our forefathers, violating the teachings of our Lord and our own consciences.

Slowly, since 1954, we have felt the first of these selves dying away and the other growing. We have experienced some release of conscience, but also a heightened anxiety about how to cope with our new situation. Consequently, we have done nothing but think and occasionally pray.

We can say of the Negroes of our community that they have sought and found sympathetic help from the white members of our church and community. Over the years an attitude of good-will has prevailed between the two communities. But now, in the second half of the century, we suddenly find ourselves living with *two* Negro communities. One is as familiar to us as our own families, the other as strange as foreigners.

The first and larger group is composed of older Negro citizens. By older I mean those who are adult, married, working members of the community. They remain relatively unchanged and look upon the recent developments affecting their race with even greater confusion and fear than do white citizens. They would much prefer to continue their dependence upon the white community for leadership and care. They appear unable and, indeed, unwilling to assume either the privileges or responsibilities of first-class citizenship. With this group there is no new problem, only the continuing problems to which we have become calloused.

The second group of Negro citizens is one which most of us have not even met. If so, we were not conscious of it. For the most part, we think of them only when we read our newspapers or hear the news reports. But they are here in Huntersville. They are educated, ambitious, and, most significant of all, they think of themselves as first-class American citizens. These young folk have breathed the invigorating air of independence and self-sufficiency.

In spirit, they are much like our pioneer forefathers. For some of them this new status has been a heady wine; for others it has been a sobering fear. While the legal machinery of the Justice Department has given them in six years the basic rights and privileges of first-class citizenship, it will take decades for them to assume the responsibilities that go along with these privileges.

On the national scene this group has gotten its finest leadership from churchmen of their own race. Yet, ironically, in our local situation they tend to look down on the church. They look down on it because they consider it uneducated, unsophisticated, and out-of-date. They see it as controlled by the older Negroes, as not facing up to the brand-new set of problems faced by the younger generation.

For example, rather than introduce the Christian viewpoint of dating, courtship, and marriage into the increasing social activities of the schools, the churches have tended generally to condemn all social functions, with the result that we are faced with an alarming number of social problems in the high school. The same deficiencies of practical religion apply to the remainder of the lives of youth in the church.

Who, then, is going to take the lead in guiding these young folk into responsible citizenship? While in school, their teachers will probably have to supply the answers; but these teachers do not live in Huntersville. They commute from Charlotte. There are few resident Negro adults who are capable alone of giving this kind of responsible leadership. In years past the responsible white citizens have supplied this need. But these patterns are no longer adequate. They do not want ready-made decisions and advice. Nor is the answer to be found in taking hands off and hoping that the answers will come automatically. This would be like a farmer waiting to work his crop until the fall.

What, then, is the solution? Quite frankly, on the practicing level I do not know what the specific answers will be. There is only one thing of which I am sure: when we find the answers it will be in the area of *cooperation*. This will not be an easy course for either the white or the Negro communities. It will be difficult for us in that it will require us to see the Negro with an entirely new attitude. We will have to see him as an intelligent and capable neighbor. It will be difficult for them because, for the most part, it will be an entirely new experience.

It will not be done quickly or easily. To attempt an easy solution is sheer sentimentality. BUT, and I cannot say this too strongly, IT MUST BE DONE AND IT MUST BEGIN NOW. Not only that, it must be initiated by the white community and, more specifically, by the church—this church.

On the national level, in these six years the Negroes have acted and the white people have reacted. The results have not made us proud of our race. This *must not* be the case in our community. So far it has been a legal battle, and we have been represented in the headlines mostly by hoodlums and mobs.

I feel strongly that as Christian citizens who occupy a privileged position of responsibility, we must seize the initiative and guide the process in a sane and sober course. Especially, as a leading church in this community, it is imperative that we give constructive guidance to our community because the only principles that offer a solution are Christian principles. If we do not employ them, who will? And if no one does, what then?

*Some Practical Policies.* I want to propose the following policies as our first action in finding the true solutions to this situation. I believe these proposals to be consistent with the gospel of Jesus Christ and our own consciences. They are intended to give some positive identification to this church as a representative of the Body of Christ in this community and to give concrete guidance to those who look to the church for instruction.

1. That the sanctuary of our church is to be considered the "house of prayer for all peoples." Those whom God has not hesitated to create in his own image and to elect to eternal fellowship with him are not to be despised by those others of us whom God has similarly regarded.

2. That, while it is hoped the worship of God will not be undertaken for any less reason than for its own noble ends, we are not ordinarily able to judge others' motives for seeking to worship. Thus, the ushers are to seat all who appear for worship and not to interfere with their worship so long as their conduct is respectful to the worship of God.

3. That, for the time being, if members of the Negro race appear for worship, they be seated with an elder and his family whenever possible. This is not to make any distinction between worshipers, but to assure the friendly acceptance of the visitor.

4. That Sunday school classes, Women of the Church, and Men of the Church organizations be urged to seek every constructive means to establish cooperation with our Negro neighbors to help them find the citizenship they seek.

5. That the members of this church consider the social, cultural, economic, moral, and religious problems of the Negro community as one with their own, realizing that the solutions can now be found only on a community-wide basis.

6. That the leaders of our church, especially the session and diaconate, seek means to cooperate in building up the integrity and witness of the Negro churches in our community without diminishing the responsibility of their officers and congregations.

7. That membership in our church be based on "belief in the Lord Jesus Christ as the Son of God and the Saviour of sinners."

8. That members of this church be especially aware of opportunities to encourage responsible Negro leadership in community affairs.

9. Finally, that we use the divine fellowship of prayer to broaden our imaginations, deepen our concerns, and strengthen our consciences as we carry out these responsibilities.

*Practice.* What does all this mean in practice? It means we must recognize that the South is changing. Old patterns are being broken, never again to be restored. An entirely new type of citizen is emerging to find his place in society, and we must somehow prepare for his coming.

It means we must be continually re-examining our Christian faith to find in it the courage and wisdom we need. We must not retreat into rigid resistance or stoic resentment, but must deal constructively with the problems before us. Only then can God work through the church to establish his will. In short, it means we have been chosen to be born in a time when something unprecedented is about to happen in history. By the grace of God, the privileged race in a society has undertaken the responsibility of lifting another race to its own level, sharing with them the privileges of its citizenship and cooperating with them in assuming its responsibilities. Only the spirit of Jesus Christ can accomplish this.

It means that we may be the first people in the human race to understand fully the meaning of praying, "Our Father who art in heaven . . ."

# Discipleship and the Church

David M. Currie
First Presbyterian Church, Durham, North Carolina
May 10, 1964

Almost exactly one year before the preaching of the following sermon, Durham, North Carolina, was enduring massive street demonstrations by some three thousand of its Negro citizens. For a desperate
three-day period, this small city of 80,000, famous for tobacco and
Duke University, seemed on the verge of martial law. Then, in a series
of rapid actions initiated by a newly elected mayor, a committee of
local business and political leaders helped the community to desegregate most of its business and municipal establishments, all within
about two weeks. Describing the work of this committee, its only
clerical member later testified: "It is fair to say that each white man
on the committee has taken a more forthright position in the community than he has in the church where he holds membership." Said one
deacon of this pastor's own congregation, "I am ready to go ahead in
my business. . . . I will be glad to employ Negroes on our staff. But I
tell you one thing: there is no use asking these questions in the
church."[1]

One year later a small but very concrete refutation of that blanket
indictment had sounded in Durham: the First Presbyterian Church
admitted a Negro member. The congregation is an old Durham institution, founded in 1871, located downtown, with a varied spectrum of
professional, business, university, sales, and other occupations represented in its present membership of 920. As early as 1957 the session
of the church adopted a policy of seating Negroes for worship without
segregation. As a result, the "kneel-ins" which preceded and accompanied the demonstrations of 1963 did not precipitate an internal congregational crisis.

The congregation came closer to crisis, however, when on Sunday,

146

May 3, 1964, in response to the minister's regular invitation to persons "moved by the Holy Spirit to desire membership in this one of Christ's congregations," four persons came to meet with the session, one of them a Negro high school student named Ronald Boyd. Mr. Currie, pastor of the church since January, 1963, describes the event as follows:

"When asked how he came to his decision, Mr. Boyd responded to the session that he had attended the city-wide Presbyterian Youth Activities Week held in this church in August, 1963; that he had worshiped with us several times, and that he came in response to the invitation as given. After an inquiry concerning his willingness to receive communicant instruction from the pastor, the session heard Mr. Boyd's profession of faith, admitted him to baptism, and received him into membership without audible dissent.

"By evening rumors and garbled information abounded. By midweek it was judged wise to send to the congregation a letter stating what had happened at the session meeting the previous Sunday. The letter included a citation of Matthew 16:13-26 as the text for next Sunday's sermon. Members were requested to read and pray over this text, and to come to worship the next Sunday.

"In the ensuing months, this young person has taken full part in the life of the congregation. One member has asked that his own name be removed from the roll. Some members publicly declared that they could not worship here any longer, but most have returned. On the other hand, one wrote to say that at last he could hold his head high as a Christian after thirty years of shame."

The sermon was preached on Ascension Sunday, adds Mr. Currie, "when things were up in the air!" The hymns sung during the service, like the sermon, gave an unmistakable witness to who it is, in history and beyond history, that enables the church to move in and beyond civil rights: "I Greet Thee, Who My Sure Redeemer Art," and "In Christ There Is No East or West."

## TEXT: MATTHEW 16:13-26

Profound actions and reactions have stirred within the life of this congregation during the last seven days. It is incumbent upon disciples of Jesus that these actions and reactions be seen in the light of the will and Word of Jesus Christ who alone is head of the church. To that end I have asked you, through a letter last week, to read and pray over the text, Matthew 16:13-26.

Three points of emphasis will be drawn from this text today:

(1) The church is Jesus'—he is its builder and Lord.

(2) Persons upon whom and through whom Jesus builds the church are fallible.

(3) Discipleship within the church is costly—but richly rewarding.

Consider with me the words of Jesus: I will build *my* church. You, as disciples of Jesus, must clearly understand that you are neither patrons nor proprietors of the church. You are not patrons of Jesus through your gifts of money, time, or life given to church-building. Jesus is never the object of your largesse; you are ever the recipients of his grace and bounty. Neither do you as disciples have a franchise to operate the church in behalf of Jesus and yourselves. No disciples of Jesus are ever "in business for themselves" with the only obligation to Jesus that of paying a franchise tax for the use of his patent. It is of utter importance that you hear and understand Jesus' word to Simon: *I will build my church.* The church is *his.* He is its builder, its Lord, its head. Any reference on your part to "my" church, to "our" church, is unwarranted and approaches blasphemy.

Now, in this building of his church Jesus uses disciples who have acclaimed him Lord and Savior—men and women who have entered in on pilgrimage as Simon had. And notice how the text makes clear that acknowledgment by Simon of Jesus as Lord and Savior wrought in him a change so profound that he was given a new name: Peter—"rock." Jesus addressed a question to the disciples: "Who do men say that the Son of man is?" People generally had varying opinions of who he was. Jesus addressed another question to the disciples: "Who do you say that I am?" Simon made reply: "You are the Christ, the Son of the living God."

The text evidences that such a declaration is made, not by fleshly wisdom, but upon God's self-revelation. Hear it from the Scripture: "Blessed are you, Simon Bar-Jona! For flesh and blood has not revealed this to you, but my Father who is in heaven. And I tell you, you are Peter, and on this rock I will build my church."

You who are disciples of Jesus have, like Simon, affirmed of

Jesus: You are the Christ—Savior and Lord—and this affirmation has been given you by God's self-revelation to you. And this affirmation has been accompanied in you by a change as profound as Simon's name change. This change is referred to elsewhere in the Scripture as regeneration, as dying and rising again, as putting off the old man and putting on the new. As disciples of Jesus you have entered into pilgrimage, and with you Jesus is building *his* church.

Now, one disclaimer needs to be made in the light of other Scripture: In his building of his church Jesus is not outside it. Jesus Christ himself is the chief cornerstone of the church. Jesus Christ is the head of the body, the church. Rightly understood, Jesus is building his church from within the fellowship.

So, the second emphasis from today's text: Jesus is building *his* church—using fallible persons who are disciples.

Great as is the declaration to Peter by Jesus in verses 18 and 19, "on this rock I will build my church" and "I will give you the keys of the kingdom of heaven," the text likewise sets forth the fallibility of disciples. It is to the same Peter that Jesus speaks the words in verse 23: "Get behind me, Satan! You are a hindrance to me; for you are not on the side of God, but of men." Yes, the Scripture affirms that in the building of his church Jesus finds his disciples fallible.

*Get behind me, Satan! You are a hindrance to me.* These are severe words. "Get behind me" is translating words which elsewhere refer to those who desert an allegiance, who forsake a cause. "Satan" is a transliteration of a word used to personify adversaries—any who consistently, vigorously oppose. "You are a hindrance to me" has in it the Greek word which transliterated gives us our English word: scandal. "You are a scandal to me." Most consistently, however, in the Scripture this word is translated: "Stumbling block." "Get behind me, Satan! You are a hindrance to me." These are words of Jesus to one of his disciples. And he continued: "for you are not on the side of God, but of men." A fair paraphrase of these words would be, "for you are not seeing things from the point of view of God."

See these words in their context. Simon confesses his faith in

Jesus as Lord and Savior. He receives a new name to mark his new condition and likewise receives the stirring declaration of Jesus: upon this rock I will build my church. Then this new disciple hears Jesus declare that he, Jesus, must go to Jerusalem, suffer many things, be killed, and on the third day be raised. Now Peter, the new disciple, remonstrates with his Lord: "God forbid . . . This shall never happen to you." He wishes to dissuade the Savior from his reclaiming, redeeming, reconciling mission. It is to a disciple who has forgotten the chief burden of his mission that Jesus cries: Get behind me, adversary, for you are a scandal to me, for you do not see things from the standpoint of the purpose and will of God.

Here is an amazing paradox of the church: it *is* divine and human; it is the channel of reconciliation, and yet it is not yet free from discord; it is the redeeming fellowship of the beloved, and is also the household of sinners who are saved by grace.

Finally, consider the words of Jesus in verses 24 and 25: "If any man would come after me, let him deny himself and take up his cross and follow me. For whoever would save his life will lose it, and whoever loses his life for my sake will find it."

This is Jesus' declaration to you as his disciple that if you seek to defend yourself against inconvenience, stress, and strain; if you labor only to secure your own ends and goals; if you strive for safety and security, you will perish in the attempt. It is likewise Jesus' declaration that if you as a disciple will abandon yourself in obedience to him as Lord, you will find yourself affirmed, validated, established by your Savior. The word translated "perish" in John 3:16 is the word in this text translated "lose." Jesus came in the love of God that you might not perish, or lose, but have everlasting life.

Now, this utter obedience means that you will come by earnest and diligent effort to think as nearly as possible as God thinks, to cherish as nearly as possible as God cherishes, to labor as nearly as possible as God labors. You will increase in your ability so to do through Christ's fellowship, companionship, communication, supported and enriched in the company of other disciples.

In discharge of my solemn and awesome responsibility under

Jesus to proclaim to you his Word, let me state the import of this text for you who are his disciples and members of this one of his congregations:

(1) You do not have here a church that is yours to defend, perpetuate, clutch to yourself. The church is Jesus', and he builds it as he chooses—using persons who are his disciples.

(2) Each of you individually and all of us collectively are fallible as disciples of Jesus, with the same possibility of becoming—as Peter did—a scandal, a hindrance to Jesus in his churchbuilding. Hate, fear, jealousy, self-pride, as well as misjudgment of Jesus' will, are scandalous among his disciples. The ruling elders of this congregation, together with the pastor, sought last Sunday to act under faithful obedience to Jesus as he builds *his* church. Together we endeavored not to think as men think apart from the Lordship of Jesus. When Ronald Boyd came, in response to invitation through the Holy Spirit, to profess his faith in Jesus as Savior and Lord, to request baptism for remission of his sin and the promise of regeneration, and requested membership in this one of Jesus' congregations for his nurturing and commissioning—the session voted to receive him as disciple with us.

(3) All of us together can expect the costliness of faithful discipleship to be thrust upon us now in dramatic fashion. True crosses are not fashioned by men for themselves but rather are thrust upon them by others. They are to be borne by disciples after the manner of Jesus himself: redemptively. Seeking to save ourselves, our pride, our isolation, our prejudices, or seeking to cultivate the weed of self-praise or the briars of antagonism, we will lose. But by faithful obedience to Jesus in his building of his church we will receive from him rich reward.

Up then, quit you like faithful disciples.

"Let the word of Christ dwell in you richly in all wisdom; teaching and admonishing one another in psalms and hymns and spiritual songs, singing with grace in your hearts to the Lord. And whatsoever ye do in word or deed, do all in the name of the Lord Jesus, giving thanks to God and the Father by him" (Colossians 3:16-17, K.J.V.).

# The Triumphant Life of the Poor in Spirit

Lawrence F. Haygood
Parkway Gardens Presbyterian Church, Memphis, Tennessee
June 7, 1964

Books about the church and race will no longer need to be printed on the day when it is no longer relevant to record that a certain Christian congregation is "all Negro." Founded in 1952 by Memphis Presbytery and located in a changing urban residential neighborhood, the Parkway Gardens Presbyterian Church represents some progress toward such a day. About eighty-five percent of the congregation's members are professionals—physicians, dentists, insurance executives, businessmen, nurses, and secretaries. Many of these members have been in the mainstream of the effort to desegregate the public institutions of Memphis[1] through energetic participation in the most effective civil rights organization in the city, the NAACP. The four top officers of the local chapter are members of the Parkway Gardens Church, and several members have served on the city-wide biracial committee.

"Memphis has the largest number of registered Negro voters of any major southern city," says Mr. Haygood, "and they played an important role in the recent presidential election. Likewise, the Negro voters were largely responsible for electing a Negro to the State House of Representatives for the first time since Reconstruction. In addition, a Negro was elected to the Shelby County Court for the first time since the early beginning of the twentieth century. And, even before the Civil Rights Act of 1964, it could be said that Memphis was a desegregated city. We are now working to make it an integrated city."

The sermon below was preached one month before the passage of the Civil Rights Act, and on June 9 it was also delivered at an integrated meeting of Presbyterian church women from the Synod of Alabama—the first such meeting sponsored by that synod. It offers convincing testimony to the truth affirmed by several other spokesmen in this collection—that out of his experience of suffering, the Negro Christian brings to the church a unique sensitivity to the gospel of the Cross.

## TEXT: MATTHEW 5:3

Who are the poor in spirit? First of all, they are those who feel deeply their spiritual helplessness; those who are aware that there is a spiritual emptiness in their lives that they cannot fill themselves; those who acknowledge that there is a deep void within themselves that can only be filled by God.

To be spiritually helpless is to stand before the presence of God empty-handed; stripped of every disguise, pleading for the compassion and mercy of Christ. Like Isaiah of old, we cry aloud, "Woe is me! For I am lost; for I am a man of unclean lips, and I dwell in the midst of a people of unclean lips; for my eyes have seen the King, the LORD of hosts!" (Isaiah 6:5).

Most of us are made constantly aware of our spiritual helplessness. Sometimes we are made aware of it after we have worked hard on a particular project or accomplishment. We give ourselves untiringly and diligently to the task that is before us. We accomplish what we set out to do. After completing the task, we receive the usual compliments from our friends and acquaintances, and we enjoy what they have to say. Yet, after the period of elation has ceased, there comes upon our lives a deep spiritual void that neither the satisfaction of having finished the job nor the kind words of friends can fill. Then we cry out, "Search me, O God, and know my heart! Try me and know my thoughts! And see if there be any wicked way in me [and there is!], and lead me in the way everlasting!" (Psalm 139:23-24). And at this Christ says to us, "Happy are those who are spiritually helpless, for theirs is the kingdom of heaven."

Moreover, the poor in spirit are the oppressed people of God who, in spite of oppression, maintain an unquenchable faith in him. Although injustice seems to be victorious, falsehood appears to triumph, hatred appears to be winning over love; nevertheless, the poor in spirit continue seeking after God for liberation, knowing that God's will will ultimately overpower and supersede the will of man.

Today the spotlight is on the Negro in America. He suffers injustices throughout the United States of America because he happens to have a dark complexion. He is oppressed in such a fashion that many doors are closed to him, even doors that are supposed to be a part of the kingdom in which he lives and labors. His daughters are killed by the hands of vicious men while they study the word of Jesus from the cross of Calvary: "Father, forgive them; for they know not what they do."[2] His sons are shot down as they ride bikes down a public street in a hate-filled city. His most courageous leaders are mowed down from behind, and his most ardent supporters are shot through the head because they happen to be sympathizing with his condition and desire to share his lot. Yet through it all, he continues to manifest the intensity of his faith in God and the seriousness of his trust in the Lord of all life. Jesus says to him: "Happy are those who are oppressed and who, despite their oppression, maintain an active faith in God and his Son, Jesus Christ, for to them belongs the Kingdom of God."

Again, the poor in spirit are the "renounced in spirit": those who have given up the notion that they can do anything at all for their inner contentment and stability; those who find life by losing it.

The disciples were all too familiar with the philosophy of the Roman world. Here was a world of wealth and a world of power; a world of culture and a world of refinement. In this culture the happy man was the man who held his brothers under bondage; the man who cared only for himself; the man who grasped for power; the man who was frustrated and despondent. Nietzsche sums up this philosophy when he tells us: "Assert yourself. Care for nothing except yourself. The only vice is weakness, and the only virtue is strength. Be strong. Be a superman. The world is yours and you can get it." This is the philosophy that Hitler embraced and carried out during his lifetime. Such a conviction drove him to feel that he could conquer the world, and he was willing to perform inhuman acts in order to do it. Someone has said, "The genesis of this philosophy is selfishness, and its exodus is suicide." The Roman Empire passed away; and Hitler was defeated; but the words of Jesus have stood the test of time: "Happy are the renounced in spirit, for theirs is life at its highest and best."

The renounced in spirit know that the way to self-fulfillment is by way of self-denial; the way to find life is to lose it. They have found life by letting it go. Jesus said, "If any man would come after me, let him deny himself and take up his cross and follow me" (Matthew 16:24). To deny oneself is to reject utterly the right to live; for "when Christ calls a man, he bids him come and die."[3] He is called to die to himself and allow Christ to take total and complete control of his being.

The modern church has lost much of its influence in the world today because it has strayed from the principles of its King. Instead of being renounced in spirit, it has become the puffed-up in spirit. Instead of losing its life, it has sought to save its life. Instead of becoming the light of the world, it has become absorbed in the darkness of the world. Erich Fromm, in commenting on religion in America today, said, "What at one time was a dynamic structure, mediating between man and his destiny and interpersonal responsibilities, has become mere mechanical ritual that dwarfs men rather than strengthens them."[4] Dr. Fromm senses that the church, instead of imparting to its communicants the spiritual resources for transforming the world, has given them shabby excuses for not becoming involved in the going-on-ness of history; flimsy alibis for not becoming creative participants in the civilizing process.

Those who have not joined the company of the renounced in spirit are suffering from spiritual paralysis, ecclesiastical complacency, religious psychosis, and soul-depressing neurosis. Indeed, they are filled with despondency, disillusionment, fear, and frustration. Life has no purpose for them, and they walk helplessly between the expressways of meaninglessness and the boulevards of nothingness. In their periods of great void and emptiness, they cry aloud that there is no happiness in this life. There is nothing but depression and despair. Life is no more than a vacuum of unfulfilled dreams and aspirations. The best that life can bring is defeat, heartbreak, and disappointment.

The renounced in spirit are happy because they have let loose on life, because they claim no existence of themselves. They have accepted sorrow, defeat, trouble, disappointments, suffering, and persecution as a part of their existence for the sake of him who has already accepted defeat. One cannot break a man who has accepted his brokenness. One cannot persecute a man who has accepted persecution as a way of life. One cannot kill a man who has already died. A man is not free until he accepts Christ's command to die to the self. "Happy are the renounced in spirit, for theirs is life at its highest and best."

Finally, the poor in spirit are humble-minded. The humble person is one who, in total dependence upon God, empties himself into the sufferings and concerns of his fellow man for the purpose of bringing about liberation and hope. The involvement of the humble person in the sufferings and concerns of his brothers often brings upon him rejection, slander, and persecution. Yet, the humble person is willing to accept the consequences because his ultimate concern is to unrobe the character of God in the midst of the society in which he resides.

After nights of agony and turmoil over the decision of the 1964 General Assembly of the Presbyterian Church, U. S. to hold its 1965 meeting at a church that denied Negroes the right to worship, a white minister of our denomination sought entrance to the historic Second Presbyterian Church with his Negro brother, an elder of Parkway Gardens. As they and others approached the steps of the Second Church, they were met by officers of the church who blocked the entrance to the house of God. After reading a brief statement and asking to be permitted to worship, they were told to leave. The group came to Parkway Gardens to worship God. Invited to speak to the congregation, this minister said, "For the first time, I have been turned away from the house of God. If I had gone alone, they would have accepted me. But they would not accept me with my Negro brother. Racial segregation is against the will of God. Christ died for all men, and no one should be denied the right to worship God on the basis of the color of his skin." In total and complete dependence upon God, this man emptied himself into the suffering and rejection of his brother for the purpose of bringing him liberation and hope.

Again, the elder of this church, in dependence upon God, has emptied himself into the captivity and enslavement of his white brother for the purpose of bringing about liberation and hope in his behalf. By seeking admission to the Second Church, he is attempting to save his white brother from the captivity of fear, bigotry, prejudice, and suspicion.[5] Through such humble men the cancerous sore of racial segregation and the rotten wound of racial hatred will be healed.

So the poor in spirit are those who deeply feel their spiritual helplessness and cry out for God's help; the oppressed people of God who, in spite of oppression, maintain an unquenchable faith in him; the renounced in spirit, who find life by losing it; and the humble who, in dependence upon God, empty their lives into the sufferings and concerns of their fellow man for the purpose of bringing about liberation and hope in the name of Jesus Christ. Such people, said Jesus, have a healthy state of existence which is characterized by a triumphant joy and a radiant felicity. For in living in such a fashion, God bestows upon them the Kingdom of heaven. The Kingdom of heaven is God directing and controlling the affairs of men. Our text does not say that the poor in spirit shall rule, but that God will rule through them. God is the Lord of history, and the poor in spirit are the instruments that he uses for the purpose of revealing his character and purpose to the world.

The happiness that comes with poverty of spirit is offered to us today in the name of him who was indeed poor in spirit; namely, Jesus Christ. This one died in our stead and was raised from the dead by almighty God that we might have a life of eternal significance. He is spiritually present with us in all the difficulties and perils of life. Let us embrace his presence and cling to his soul.

# On Speaking Terms with One Another

Scott McCormick, Jr.
Tyler Memorial Presbyterian Church, Radford, Virginia
June 14, 1964

The town of Radford is forty-five miles west of Roanoke in the Valley of Virginia. Its population, 10,000, is ten percent Negro. In common with many parts of the state of Virginia, the town might be described, in Dr. McCormick's words, as "quietly but deeply conservative." All schools are segregated except the high school, which has recently accepted five Negro students. Major industries (a powder plant, a weaving mill, a foundry) employ a few Negroes in semi-skilled jobs, but local merchants have yet to employ a Negro clerk. The town's largest institution is Radford College, long a teacher-training college of the state university system.

Tyler Memorial Presbyterian Church has 225 members, comprising a cross section of the white community. A large proportion of the worshiping congregation includes college students and professors, some of whom are from other countries and cultures.

No visible ripple in Radford's traditional patterns of race relations had stirred by September, 1963; but in that month Dr. McCormick took the initiative in helping to form a local Council on Human Relations. In the ensuing eighteen months the Council was instrumental in enrolling a Negro student in the local high school, establishing a college scholarship fund, registering four hundred new voters, and arranging a job-qualification canvass of the Negro community. In addition, "little groups of honesty," referred to in the sermon, have been meeting in homes of Council members. "One wants to give thanks," says Dr. McCormick, "for certain atheists, agnostics, humanists, and Jews in town who are unaffected by the negative witness of a cautious clergy in this matter. Such persons have provided some of the major leaders of the Council."

He describes the setting of the sermon for June 14, 1964, as follows: "For the past three years our weekly newspaper notice has carried a welcome to 'people of every race, station, and social position.' In the six years of my pastorate here no Negro had attended our Sunday morning service. On this particular Sunday, Mr. Edward Fleming, from Ridgeway, Virginia, was attending a conference at Radford College next door to our church; and he worshiped with us. Mr. Fleming happened to be a Negro. He was well received by the congregation, and he himself seemed to find the service very meaningful. Since then additional members have become involved in the Council on Human Relations, and a few have invited local Negro friends to attend this church. Negro citizens here are perhaps even more cautious than whites; so far, few have come. There is no doubt that our session would cordially receive a Negro applicant for membership."

Mr. Fleming, the first Negro to visit Tyler Memorial Church, was later contacted by the editor. His response, along with the sermon below, makes a hopeful conclusion to this volume: "Although I have had much exposure to integrated meetings and feel that I have some Caucasian friends, in this service of worship I suddenly became acutely aware of the meaning of the phrase 'brotherhood of man.' Here was a man and a brother! He stood upright, leading his people, giving specific instructions on a subject usually cloaked in platitudes. If this man, I thought, could possess such genuine feeling on this subject, then there must certainly be many, many more men like him. I then realized that the Negro was no longer alone in his struggle for equality and that his problem had at last become a problem for men of all races to overcome. I thanked God for Scott McCormick and prayed God's blessing on him and the many more Scott McCormicks throughout the world."

## TEXT: GENESIS 11:7; ACTS 2:6

Language is at the heart of human relations. How well or poorly it operates indicates how matters are going with men. "Smith and Brown," it may be said, "are not on good speaking terms." That is, a conflict has arisen between them, with communication thereby impaired.

Language is the ultimate in communication, defining actions and attitudes which might otherwise be misjudged. It is so even with God, whose word and deed are biblically taken to equal each other and whose decisive act in Christ is defined as the

Word-become-flesh. Jesus is God's language, the ultimate in God's conversation with man.

Now, of course, people communicate in ways other than words —a knowing look, a gentle touch, a revealing smile or nod. But when they would probe the depths together, open up new avenues of thought, come to a deeper rapport, they must then converse in so many words. Lovers, for example, could better be blind than deaf; for deafness is loneliness, isolation from what those at hand are thinking—a frustrated foreigner far removed from the only tongue he knows.

Relating to one another successfully involves speaking with one another meaningfully. And the paramount domestic question facing us now is whether we will learn to do so. I refer to the problem of race relations. Our country is on the threshold this June of what will probably be an unparalleled push for civil rights. Under the first rays of the summer sun demonstrations are being renewed, and already violence has erupted in reaction against them.

To this situation the church can ill afford to close her eyes while claiming to be God's people. Rather, we must view the situation from the vantage point of our mission to be a redemptive agent in society. We must see that our mission is to help men, all men, speak with one another successfully. And we must admit that the men of our society, among whom we church members must be numbered, are *not* on good speaking terms.

This was the problem at Babel. At first, we read, "the whole earth had one language and few words" (Genesis 11:1). Which is to say, men were meant to speak the same language, were meant to get along; and, presumably, so they would, living under God's lordship. However, the men in this story rebelled against that lordship, seeking to aggrandize themselves. "Let us make a name for ourselves," was the cry. In other words, punctuated by the Hebrew view of one's name denoting his character, "Let us determine for ourselves what we will be like!" Though God called them to be obedient creatures, they preferred to design their own names for themselves.

The outcome of this rebellion is a confusion of speech. Now

these men cannot understand one another. One is reminded of C. S. Lewis' fanciful description of hell (in *The Great Divorce*) as a place of increasingly isolated houses. It is a country whose citizens can have their houses wherever they wish, simply by *thinking* a house. But the people there cannot abide having neighbors. The more they try to make conversation, the more contentious and confusing they become. So they keep moving farther and farther apart, until astronomical distances separate them. And that is exactly the hell of it.

Such is the issue of self-centeredness. Out of harmony with God, man cannot get on with his fellows, fails to speak effectively with them. Man was not created to go it alone or to determine by himself his destiny. Created rather for existence under God, he performs efficiently only as he acknowledges his creaturehood. This, I believe, helps explain the Negro's poise in the current emotion-ridden struggle. He has a sense of amity with God, a sense of God's being in this thing with him, and thus is able to maintain an amazing degree of dignity in the face of insults and hostile force. The Negro's enemies, on the other hand, have often initiated ill-bred vehemence against peaceful demonstrators, have pushed the panic button, perhaps because they sense that Providence is working against them.

The truth is that disharmony with God leads inevitably to disharmony among men. History stands to admonish us: When men resolve to shape their future in opposition to God's will for them, confusion and chaos ensue. That is just how it is in God's moral order.

One needs no genius to recognize this truth in the church's failings in race relations. At the local level she has been not so much a significant voice for remedial action as another confusing tongue. For years now she has been sacrificing clear obedience to God's Word in the interest of sustaining a "respectable" appearance and a "successful" program. We have professed a love for the Negro, a concern for his person and welfare; but in waging the war for Suburbia and hoping to keep open our access roads to wealth, we have done cautiously little to encourage the Negro to become a full member of society. We have clouded many of our grand pro-

nouncements with closed doors on Sunday and with pleas for
"more time" to set things right. Endeavoring thus to determine or
protect her own destiny, the church has generated a colossal confusion. Not only is she largely unable to converse with the world,
much of which has turned away in disillusionment to humanistic
thought and institutions for inspiration and action; she cannot
even converse with herself too well. Her members are speaking
different languages regarding race relations. There is no small
misunderstanding within the house of God.

I do not say the church has made no progress in the last few
years. She *has* made progress, for which any sane man can be
grateful. Still, we dupe ourselves if we suppose that Babel's confusion is behind us now. We are not communicating as we should
with the Negro, who is perplexed with our preachments of
love every time a door is slammed in his face. Nor are we communicating sensibly among ourselves when we speak courageously
in generalities but cower before specifics. There is confusion in
the land; there is confusion in the church.

Contrasting the confusion that Babel means is the significance
of Pentecost. Pentecost is the redemptive sequel to Babel, as if
the same hand wrote both narratives. Note the directly opposing
details.

At Babel men are concerned with their own accomplishments
—a city and a tower to get themselves a name; but at Pentecost
the concern is with God's accomplishments: his "mighty works"
are proclaimed. Accordingly, while the men in the Babel story act
under their own power, those at Pentecost speak empowered of
the Holy Spirit. The one group is taken with self, the other taken
by God. Further, the nations are scattered at Babel but at Pentecost are brought together. Finally and most apparently, men at
Babel do not understand what others are saying, but at Pentecost
everyone understands.

What is the meaning of the Pentecost-event? Existentially for
us it is this: *In Christ the basic problem of language is solved.* Men
can speak intelligibly, can relate to one another harmoniously, in
that they are harmoniously related to God. The sin of a hopeless
self-centeredness which once stood as a wall between them has

mercifully been removed. No longer is it an impenetrable barrier to communication. Rather, in Christ, the Second Adam, a new humanity is brought into being. In him men are graciously put back on good speaking terms. Sensible, redemptive, interpersonal relations are a possibility for us. The outpouring of the Spirit at Pentecost set that possibility into powerful motion. Though imperfect themselves, the Christians at Pentecost could speak an intelligible word—a word which the world could hear and at least somewhat understand; a word centered in God's mighty acts, cutting right through human confusion and offering meaningful existence to all. In Christ the basic problem of language, the problem of broken human relations, meets its solution. In him the Tower of Babel comes crashing down. We do not *have* to be hopelessly confusing, do not *have* to be ruled by self-seeking and chaos, do not *have* to yield to either determinism or despair in any of their pessimistic forms. There is in Christ a power at hand to re-create and use us.

It remains now to direct this specifically to the church's mission in race relations. That the church has for men in conflict a word of reconciliation is clear enough. What concerns me is the church's proclivity to get in the way of reconciliation. The embarrassing fact is that we ourselves need it. Being so much a product of our environment, we often exert a negative effect, even though our intent for better race relations may be more sincere than some people think. We have the reconciling word, yes, but we may be frustrating the Spirit's work of reconciliation just by the way we attempt to share in it.

The church's behavior at Pentecost suggests three necessary factors in a vital proclamation of that word. The first is that the word must be spoken where the people are. Peter and his colleagues were in a house when the Spirit rushed upon them to loose their tongues, and soon the Spirit had them outside the house, where their preaching could be heard. Odd, perhaps, that this necessity should have to be stressed. But the church has holed up with her powerful word and is preaching mainly—sometimes only—to herself. The world is not in here nor, for the most part, is likely to enter even upon invitation. We must therefore get out in the street, where the traffic is. Merely to stay inside would be a denial of the reality and implications of the Incarnation!

This requirement is all the more crucial in that the very people with whom we white Christians need to be reconciled have been, both literally and figuratively, put out in the street by us. It is all very proper for us to say that we want to be on good speaking terms with the Negro and that he would be welcomed if he appeared here Sunday morning—but *he* is not too sure of that. He has not exactly been swamped with greetings from white individuals or with invitations to attend such gatherings as their personal guests.

Do we want to learn to speak with the Negro as reconciled brothers in Christ? show him we do believe God's grace can break down the barriers to communication? speak to him a word not garbled by static? Then we shall have to get out in the street where the man is—stand next to him, shoulder to shoulder, yes, in a demonstration and wherever else we find him.

Secondly, our preaching of reconciliation must be done in obvious concern for the welfare of those addressed. The fact that these Pentecost preachers were out in the midst of the multitude was clear evidence that they cared. And their concern was not merely a so-called "spiritual" one, limited to the state of men's "souls." It was a total concern, viewing the needs of those men then and there—the need for forgiveness, the need for fellowship, the need for friendship, the need for food. Soon after Peter's Pentecost sermon the early Christians established a community of sharing. They worshiped, visited, broke bread together. And they called that community the church!

So also must you and I communicate a lively concern. There are Negroes in this city, some of whom you know by name, who regard the white man's announced concern for them, *your* concern for them, with a chuckle at best. They are polite to you and generally put up a front of being reasonably content with their lot. But you do not know them really; you just think you know them. I have sat with them in their homes and mine in little groups of honesty. When they feel free to remove the mask, revealing something of the indescribable hurt and hell it is to be black, one may first want to argue or offer excuses; but soon one wants to cry. Beloved, we have yet to demonstrate our concern for these people in meeting them as equals, in struggling alongside them for justice, in according them civil and social respect. We have yet to speak with them as true brothers in Christ, have yet to prove our concern by simply *showing it*.

Now, granted, if we did get outside this building with God's word and declare a practical concern for the Negro's total welfare, such a preaching of reconciliation would no doubt result in difficulties for us. Even if we were as wise as serpents, we would engage opposition, would lose certain members, would lose some money as well. But there is a third necessity to consider: willingness to leave the consequences of our preaching to God.

The earliest of Christ's followers had to do so. At Pentecost they immediately encountered misjudgment in the complaint, "These men are drunk." Soon they were to meet antagonism, even persecution. But they had a word to proclaim and were given no assurances of either creaturely comforts or desirable results at any one turn. Consequences would have to be left to God.

Let us therefore lay expediency aside in the interest of a righteous, self-effacing proclamation. Let us leave the results of our witness—indeed, leave our very destiny—to him who can be trusted to see us through whatever comes our way. And let us ask ourselves whether we have been speaking and whether we will be speaking, in deed and in truth, the word which cuts through Babel's confusion and enables men themselves to speak with one another.

To this there is only the answer:

Our Father, who art in heaven, hallowed be thy name. Thy Kingdom come. Thy will be done on earth as it is in heaven. Give us this day our daily bread. And forgive us our debts, as we forgive our debtors. And lead us not into temptation, but deliver us from evil: For thine is the Kingdom, and the power, and the glory, for ever. Amen.

# NOTES

*Introduction*

1. Ernest Q. Campbell and Thomas F. Pettigrew, *Christians in Racial Crisis: A Study of Little Rock's Ministry* (Washington, D. C.: Public Affairs Press, 1959), Preface, p. viii.

2. In these two respects it differs from the other major southern regional denomination—the Southern Baptist Convention. From 1931 to 1940, however, by vote of their General Assembly, southern Presbyterians did withdraw from the National Council's predecessor, the Federal Council of Churches.

3. See H. Richard Niebuhr, *The Meaning of Revelation* (New York: The Macmillan Company, 1941), p. 64.

4. Minutes of the One-Hundred-Fifth General Assembly of the Presbyterian Church in the U.S. (1965), Part II, p. 128.

5. Minutes of the Ninety-Fourth General Assembly (1954), Part I, p. 193.

6. This statement is partly impressionistic and partly based on the evidence of the one hundred twenty-five sermons considered for inclusion in this volume.

7. For a thorough description of the background and content of this doctrine, see Ernest Trice Thompson, *The Spirituality of the Church* (Richmond: John Knox Press, 1961).

8. See *ibid.*, p. 11, and the same author's *Presbyterians in the South* (Richmond: John Knox Press, 1963), Vol. I, pp. 93-96.

9. See Martin Luther King, "Letter from a Birmingham Jail" (Philadelphia: American Friends Service Committee, p. 12), reprinted in Martin Luther King, *Why We Can't Wait* (New York: The New American Library of World Literature, Inc., 1964), p. 91.

10. *The Westminster Confession of Faith*, Chapter V, paragraph 1.

11. A. S. P. Woodhouse, *Puritanism and Liberty* (Chicago: University of Chicago Press, 1951), Introduction, p. 42.

12. *Ibid.*, pp. 38-42.

13. Acts 26:26.

## THE AUTHORITY OF THE WORD

*Amos Diagnoses Our Southern Sickness*

1. As reported in *Southern School News*, Vol. IV, No. 1 (July, 1957), p. 4.

2. *Ibid.*, Vol. IV, No. 2 (August, 1957), p. 13.

3. *Ibid.*

4. *South Carolinians Speak* (no publisher given), p. 73.

5. *Ibid.*, p. 23.

### And in Samaria?

1. Ben Lacy Rose, *Racial Segregation in the Church,* reprinted from *The Presbyterian Outlook* (Outlook Publishers, Richmond, Va., 1957), p. 4.

2. Joachim Jeremias, *Jesus' Promise to the Nations,* Studies in Biblical Theology, No. 24 (London: SCM Press Ltd., 1958), pp. 42-43. The Greek word used by Professor Jeremias is here given the English form, 'Samaritan.'

3. David Head, *He Sent Leanness* (New York: The Macmillan Company, 1959), p. 43.

4. Elizabeth Bowne, *Gift from the African Heart* (New York: Dodd, Mead and Company, 1961), p. 186.

### No Back Doors in Heaven

1. Ben Lacy Rose, *Racial Segregation in the Church,* p. 20.

### Foundations

1. The other two are the downtown First Church and the Brown Memorial Church, located near the Stillman campus and organizationally related not to Tuscaloosa Presbytery but to a separate presbytery for Negro churches.

2. The Brown Memorial Church and two others. See statistics on southern Presbyterian "Negro" churches in editor's preface to Mr. Lowry's sermon, "I Have a Dream."

3. Minutes of the One-Hundred-Fourth General Assembly (1964), Part I, pp. 80-81.

4. *The Book of Church Order,* §2-1.

#### CIVIL DISORDER

### Not Race But Grace

1. See James 1:5-6 (K.J.V. and R.S.V.).

2. Quoted by Donald M. Baillie, *Out of Nazareth* (New York: Charles Scribner's Sons, 1958), pp. 36-37.

3. Revelation 19:6.

### Love Disqualified

1. Sermon copyrighted 1963 by the Christian Century Foundation. Reprinted by permission from *The Pulpit,* February, 1963.

### The Testing of Our Faith

1. Geographically and economically, it has much in common with Marion and Mullins. See the editor's preface to Mr. Lyles' sermon, "Amos Diagnoses Our Southern Sickness," and Mr. DuBose's sermon, "My Home Town."

2. At the time of the Revolutionary War, Fayetteville (then the twin towns of Cross Creek and Campbell Town) was the largest settlement of Scotch Highlanders in America. See E. T. Thompson, *Presbyterians in the South,* p. 36.

### Christian Response to Racial Revolution

1. Henry F. Lyte, "Abide with Me" (1820).

2. James Henley Thornwell, leading minister and educator of South Carolina in the pre-Civil War decades, when "more than any other he molded and reflected the mind of Southern Presbyterianism." See E. T. Thompson, *Presbyterians in the South,* Vol. I, p. 498.

3. Romans 8:28 (K.J.V.).

CIVIL RIGHTS

*The March on Washington*

1. E. T. Thompson, *Presbyterians in the South,* Vol. I, pp. 93-96.

2. *The Presbyterian Outlook,* Vol. 145, No. 33 (September 23, 1963), pp. 5-7, under the title "Our Duty in the Racial Crisis." Permission to reprint it here has been given by *The Presbyterian Outlook.* It may also be noted that support of the March on Washington was given by the General Board of the National Council of Churches at its midsummer meeting in 1963, and that only Presbyterian U.S. representatives to the Board openly excepted themselves from this support. Southern Presbyterians who did participate in the March, then, did so under the implied disapproval of the only denominational leaders who had occasion to speak officially on the subject.

*I Have a Dream*

1. Statistics were obtained from the Board of Church Extension of the Presbyterian Church, U.S. and are accurate as of October, 1964.

2. In Kentucky on the synod, state-wide level, the two denominations are in many respects one organization. A large number of common programs are carried on—in the fields of church school training, college and seminary institutions, and various planning committees.

3. Matthew 5:48 (K.J.V.).

*Capitulation to Caesar*

1. See editor's preface to Mr. Lowry's sermon, "I Have a Dream."

2. "Pastor's Word," *The Redeemer,* monthly publication of the Church of the Redeemer, Vol. IV, No. 2 (December, 1964), p. 8.

3. Karl Barth, *Against the Stream* (London: SCM Press Ltd., 1954), pp. 22-23.

4. Harry S. Ashmore, *An Epitaph for Dixie* (New York: W. W. Norton & Company, Inc., 1958), pp. 170, 179 (italics ours).

*The Maker of Peace*

1. Robert Frost, "Mending Wall," in *Complete Poems of Robert Frost* (New York: Holt, Rinehart and Winston, Inc., 1949). This sermon opened with larger excerpts from "Mending Wall," of which this is the first line.

2. John Greenleaf Whittier, "Maude Muller," in *The Complete Poetical Works of Whittier* (New York: Houghton Mifflin Company, 1894), p. 47.

3. John Milton, "Samson Agonistes," in *The Complete Poetical Works of John Milton* (New York: Houghton Mifflin Company, 1941), p. 445.

4. Arthur Miller, *Death of a Salesman* (New York: The Viking Press, 1949).

5. Sophocles, *Oedipus Coloneus,* tr. R. C. Jebb (New York: Cambridge University Press, 1885), pp. 192-193.

6. Trade name of Atlanta restaurant operator Lester Maddox, who rejected Negro customers at gunpoint, resulting in the first test case of the Civil Rights Bill.

*God's Agents*

1. Sermon reprinted here, by permission, from *The Presbyterian Outlook* (Vol. 46, No. 39, pp. 5-6), where it appeared in the issue of November 2, 1964, under the title "What Is the Church's Mission?"

2. Quoted from "The National Council of Churches and the Mississippi Summer Project at a Glance," Office of Information, National Council of Churches, July 8, 1964.

BEYOND CIVIL RIGHTS

*Discipleship and the Church*

1. Warren Carr, "Notes from an Irrelevant Clergyman," *The Christian Century,* Vol. LXXX, No. 28 (July 10, 1963), pp. 879-880.

*The Triumphant Life of the Poor in Spirit*

1. See editor's preface to Dr. Jones's sermon, "God's Agents."

2. The Sunday school lesson at Birmingham's Sixteenth Street Baptist Church on September 15, 1963, was entitled "Love That Forgives."

3. Dietrich Bonhoeffer, *The Cost of Discipleship* (London: SCM Press Ltd., 1959), p. 79.

4. From a conversation recorded by Chandler Brossard, "A Visit with Erich Fromm," *Look* Magazine, Vol. 28, No. 9 (May 5, 1964), p. 56.

5. In January, 1965, the Moderator of the General Assembly took action to change the meeting place of the 1965 Assembly from the Second Church of Memphis to Montreat, North Carolina.